DAUGHTERS OF AFRICA

A QUEEN MOTHER IN ASHANTI.

(Her robe is of deep blue silk with a rich pattern of gold. Her ornaments are of
gold also ; so is the beautiful woven band round her forehead.)

DAUGHTERS OF
AFRICA

BY

G. A. GOLLOCK

*WITH PORTRAITS, ILLUSTRATIONS
AND A MAP*

NEGRO UNIVERSITIES PRESS
NEW YORK

Originally published in 1932
by Longmans, Green and Co., London

Reprinted 1969 by
Negro Universities Press
A DIVISION OF GREENWOOD PUBLISHING CORP.
NEW YORK

SBN 8371-1765-8

PRINTED IN UNITED STATES OF AMERICA

TO THE
HUSBANDS AND SONS
OF
DAUGHTERS OF AFRICA

PREFACE

DAUGHTERS OF AFRICA is the third book of stories written for young Africans who are stepping out into life after leaving school or college. Dr. J. E. K. Aggrey, who contributed so much to the first two volumes, has also left his mark on this. Long talks with him led me to share his views about women of African race. As a guest in his American home I saw how his ideals worked out in life.

He was passionately proud of the women of his race, of their capacity, their devotion as wives and mothers, their unflagging work in the cultivation of the soil and the provision of food for the family. I can see the flash of his eye as he urged that no education was too good for a woman of Africa. Given opportunity in the new day, he believed that she would render as large service to her country as did women in lands of the West.

The stories told in this book are true and are full of human interest. In the case of some of the younger women the actual names have not been given. Such stories of African women have apparently never been issued in a book before. What is published here is only a small part of what was sent from all parts of Africa by men and women of many races and callings in response to a single personal request from the author. Some of the help so generously given is acknowledged on the opposite page. In several cases stories awaiting future publication were sent by their writers with leave to use them, either recast or as they stood. Life stories written by Africans themselves add interest and value to the book. Some charming tales were found in old records in the library of the Royal Empire Society.

The manuscript was submitted, in whole or in part, to readers with specialised African knowledge, who have given valuable help. The Rev. E. W. Smith, author of *The Golden Stool*, has, with his wonted generosity, read the whole book in proof.

The Phelps-Stokes Fund, at the instance of Canon Anson Phelps Stokes and Dr. T. Jesse Jones, has made it possible to set aside the time required for the study of *Daughters of Africa*.

One small foretaste of the contents of the book may be given here. A month's " refresher course " was being held at San Salvador in the Portuguese Congo. Some sixty African teachers and twenty of their wives came in from the surrounding districts. Several of the wives shared in the lectures given to the men. One day the subject of how to teach arithmetic was under discussion. The lecturer began : " If the Portuguese school inspector appeared suddenly in your schoolroom and bid you give an arithmetic lesson in his presence, what would you do ? " There was silence for a moment. Then an African teacher spoke. " I would call my wife," he said.

G. A. GOLLOCK.

LONDON,
June, 1932.

ACKNOWLEDGMENTS

STORY material from the following correspondents, among many others, has been gratefully used :

WEST AFRICA. Mrs. Arnot (Arochuku), fine stories generously given; Miss Bean (Onitsha) ; Rev. H. Carter (S. Rhodesia) ; Miss Coppin (San Salvador) ; Nurse Jewitt (Isoko) ; Rev. S. Kingston (S. Nigeria) ; Mrs. Melville Jones (Lagos) ; Mrs. Palmer (Yalemba, Belgian Congo) ; Miss Spurr (Ijebu Ode) ; Mrs. Wakeman (Lagos) ; Mrs. E. F. E. Wilkinson (Ebu Owerri), much good material given.

EAST AND CENTRAL AFRICA. Archdeacon Daniell (Uganda) ; Dr. and Mrs. A. R. Cooke (Uganda) ; Miss Gathercole (Likoma) ; Miss Heywood (Nairobi) ; Mrs. Mackenzie (Nyasaland) ; Herr Otto Raum (Marangu, Tanganyika) ; Misses Roe, Daws, and Dutton (Masasi) ; Rev. G. Sketchley (S. Rhodesia) ; Mrs. Syson (Elgon).

SOUTH AFRICA. The Bishop of St. Albans (Pretoria) ; Mrs. F. B. Bridgman (Johannesburg), a wealth of varied help ; Miss Cooke (Ladysmith) ; Mrs. Cowles (Umzumbe, Natal), the splendid story of Noma-mbotwe ; Miss Dora Earthy (Lebombo) ; Miss Dorothy Maud (Ekatuleni, Johannesburg) ; M. de Meuron (Lausanne) ; Deaconess Vigor (Johannesburg).

AFRICAN CONTRIBUTORS include Chief Abdiele and two other Africans at Mamba, Tanganyika ; Rev. John Dube (Ohlange, Natal) ; Prof. D. D. T. Jabavu (Fort Hare, near Lovedale) ; Mrs. Oluwole (Lagos) ; Mrs. Kamba Simango (P.E.A.) ; Ruth Masinga's story (Hope Fountain, S. Rhodesia) is written by herself ; a pamphlet by Dr. Alfred Xuma (Johannesburg) has provided some material towards the story of Mrs. Maxeke.

FROM THE UNITED STATES contributions have been sent by Miss H. B. Calder (Boston : American missionaries) ; and by Mrs. L. R. Daly (Tuskegee) ; Miss P. S. Byrd (Hampton), Miss Coleman (Bishop Tuttle Memorial, Raleigh, N.C.).

BOOKS. In addition to the older records, stories have been found in Bryant, *Olden Times in Zululand and Natal* (Longmans), including material from Turnbull's *Tales from Natal ;* Dundas, *Kilimanjaro and its People* (Witherby) ; Huxley (Julian), *Africa View* (Chatto and Windus) ; Lloyd, *Highwayman and other Tales* (C.M.S.) ; Mackenzie, *The Spirit-ridden Konde* (Seeley Service) ; Murray, *The School in the Bush* (Longmans) ; Phillips, *The Bantu are Coming* (Student Movement Press); Smith, E. W., *Aggrey of Africa* (Student Movement Press) ; and Stow's classic, *Native Races in South Africa*.

CONTENTS

PART I

FROM THE PAST TO THE PRESENT

PART II

LINKING THE OLD AND THE NEW

LIST OF ILLUSTRATIONS

DAUGHTERS OF AFRICA

PART I

FROM THE PAST TO THE PRESENT

CHAPTER 1

QUEENS IN TWO AFRICAN LANDS

THIS book is full of true stories about African women. Some of them lived hundreds of years ago, others are still living. There are tales of queens and woman chiefs, of women whose names are known in history and of others who lived ordinary lives in simple homes, of women who never even learned to read as well as of those who had a good education. They are all so unlike each other that you never can guess what is coming on the next page.

The story of sons of Africa has often been told. The story of daughters of Africa is as well worth telling. Indeed, neither story is complete without the other, for boys and girls, men and women, are always influencing one another and together they shape the life of the land. Though this book is all about African women it is meant as much for African boys as for girls. A few years hence the boys and girls who are now leaving school will be husbands and wives, with a new generation of little boys and girls growing up round them to be servants of Africa.

We begin with the stories of some queens.

I

ANCIENT QUEENS IN EGYPT

Races which are neither Negro nor Bantu have founded states in Africa. In these women have often held high position as wives and mothers of kings, and even as reigning queens. Such women have been daughters of Africa by adoption if not by race. Every African girl has the right to take interest in their lives.

In the far distant past, about three thousand five hundred years ago, a queen reigned over Egypt for more than twenty years. This was a strange event in history, for Egypt was very great and powerful, with a wonderful civilisation. It was not the sort of country that would welcome a woman's rule. But QUEEN HATSHEPSUT governed her people well. Some of the buildings she raised are standing still. Pictures carved on them show the things she did. Some of her sayings are written on stone. Scholars have learned to read them, though no one now writes with the strange signs the ancient Egyptians used.

Hatshepsut loved peace rather than war. Early in her reign she built a magnificent temple for one of the gods of Egypt. She planned a beautiful garden for this temple and wished to have many myrrh trees there. So a great expedition was sent to Punt on the shores of the Red Sea, where myrrh trees grew. It is now called Somaliland. Hatshepsut had the whole story of the expedition carved in stone pictures on the temple. They can still be seen. The queen also restored some ancient temples which had been neglected. She said of herself, " I have restored that which was in ruins, I have raised up that which was unfinished." She was perhaps the first great woman of whom we have any record.

Some of the most glorious years of Egyptian history passed. Then two queens appear beside their husbands.

QUEEN TIY, the first of the two, was a woman of lowly birth. Her husband, one of the greatest kings of Egypt, was not ashamed of the fact. The parents of Tiy were honoured, her name appeared with that of the king on all the royal proclamations. He stood boldly by the woman he trusted and loved. Queen Tiy was worthy of it all. Her strong influence never failed to help and uphold her husband. When he died, having reigned for nearly thirty-six years, the queen was left as the guardian of her young son. As we follow his story we see him first with his mother, then with his mother and wife, then with his wife and little daughters, one of the most charming family groups in ancient history.

Queen Tiy held the reins of power at first. Her son's health was bad and at times he suffered greatly. While still only a boy he was married to a beautiful little girl named NEFER-TITI, daughter of a Syrian king. Queen Tiy watched over the young pair as wisely as she watched over the kingdom.

As the young king grew older his mind was filled with thoughts unlike the people of his day.

He turned away from the many gods of Egypt
with their powerful priests. He went back to the
old Egyptian love for the sun-god Aton, source of
light and heat and power. He changed his name
to Akhnaton, which meant " the glory of Aton " ;
he would not use the names of the other Egyptian

NEFER-TITI, AN EGYPTIAN QUEEN

gods. The sign which began to appear on his
monuments and pictures was the sun with rays of
light shining down upon men, each ray ending in
a hand which could touch and lay hold. Akhnaton
wrote a hymn which is like one of the most
beautiful psalms in the Bible.

The rulers of Egypt were generally proud and

distant, hiding their family life from their people. But Akhnaton made the artists show him in pictures just as he was. Five years after his marriage Nefer-titi bore him a child—not the heir to the throne for which Egypt was waiting, but a little girl. Her seven children were all girls. There are fascinating pictures of the king and the queen looking out of a window, or driving in a chariot, always with the little daughters by their side.

After some years Akhnaton and his wife moved to a new city which he built. Here Queen Tiy came to visit them in state. The family doings are told in pictures in some of the tombs. In one the king and Queen Nefer-titi and two little girls are shown with Queen Tiy. Food is heaped in luxury on tables, with masses of flowers. Akhnaton, with a bone in his hand, according to Egyptian custom, is biting off some meat. Nefer-titi has a small roast bird in her hands and is eating it. Tiy is sharing some choice bit of food with Akhnaton's youngest sister. The little princesses feed by their mother's side.

When at last the great Queen Tiy died the king buried her in a tomb near her lowly father and mother. On the great and costly coffin it is written that Akhnaton " made it for his mother."

Nefer-titi—see the picture on p. 4—was one of the most beautiful women in the ancient world. From the early days of her marriage to the close of her life she loved her royal husband as he loved her. Other Egyptian kings had more than one wife ; Akhnaton and Nefer-titi were enough for each other. Some of the stone pictures of great state gatherings show the husband and wife seated

by each other, her arm slipped round his waist.
When Akhnaton built his great new city he marked
its limits by boundary stones. The writings on
these can still be read by scholars. Here is one
sentence which reveals the secret of a royal
Egyptian home : " My heart is happy in the
queen and her children."

II

WOMEN AND THE THRONE IN ABYSSINIA

Abyssinia, or Ethiopia as its inhabitants like to
call it, is the last independent kingdom left in
Africa. It has been admitted to the membership
of the League of Nations.

Women had a large part in its long and disturbed history. One of the most attractive stories
in the Old Testament tells of the visit of the
QUEEN OF SHEBA, a country in Southern Arabia, to
Solomon, King of Israel. The meeting of the
two rulers, with all the surroundings of wealth and
glory, is like a bright and pleasing picture, full of
colour and life. All Ethiopians believe that a son
was born to the Queen of Sheba as she journeyed
home and that he became the founder of their
kingdom. He was called Menelik I. Many tales
have gathered round him, and his royal mother is
held in honour throughout the land.

Another story, just as fresh and bright in its
colour, comes in the New Testament, when the
first Christian teachers began to take their message
into the world. One of them, named Philip, was
on the desert road between Jerusalem and Gaza.
A man drove up in his chariot. Philip ran close

to the man and heard him read aloud from a familiar book—the book of Isaiah the prophet. " Do you understand what you are reading ? " asked Philip boldly. " How can I, except some one shall guide me ? " was the honest reply. A minute later Philip was beside the reader in his chariot, explaining eagerly that the words of Isaiah the prophet had all been fulfilled in Jesus Christ. Quickly the message was welcomed and understood. The man in the chariot believed with all his heart. The chariot was drawn up by some water at the wayside. Philip baptised his new-found friend and left him. The rejoicing reader went on his way. Who was he, and where did he go ?

He was an Ethiopian, in charge of all the treasure of CANDACE, queen of the land. Old historians tell us that " for her excellent qualities she left her name as an honour to all queens since." Back to his royal mistress, with a new treasure greater than all her other treasures, came the man whom Philip had met. Candace became a Christian. Thus the Good News came to Abyssinia through its queen. For many hundreds of years Abyssinia has had a national Christian Church, and has it still.

The next queen who stands out in the history of the country is JUDITH, a Jewish princess. She was a ruler of the Falasha, Jews who had hidden themselves away in the mountains and kept their old faith. But Judith was not content to be out of sight : she wanted more place and power. She led her people to revolt, killed the royal family of Ethiopia all but one, and reigned over most of Abyssinia for forty years. The baby king who was rescued from her cruelty by faithful servants was taken to Shoa in the centre of the country. He carried on the ancient line. Long after the harsh and ruinous reign of Judith was over, the descendants of the baby king who had been rescued at last returned to their rightful throne.

Within the last hundred years public affairs in Abyssinia have been influenced by several women. TAVAVICH, a daughter of one of the emperors, married a man of no distinction who became king of Ethiopia in the end. Under the name of Theodore he was recognised by all the European countries. As long as his good wife lived to guide him with her counsel all went well. Afterwards he turned to evil ways and died in defeat and misery. When Menelik II, the greatest king Abyssinia has ever known, died in 1913, he left a widow, the EMPRESS TAITU. She strove to gain influence over the young heir to the throne, a grandson of her husband. But she failed, and the young king failed. After his downfall the daughter of Menelik, ZAUDITU by name, was crowned Empress of Ethiopia in February, 1917.

Her coronation, though far outdone when her successor the present emperor of Abyssinia was crowned in 1930, was a splendid affair. She spent the night before it in the great church of St. George, where she was crowned by the Abuna (Archbishop) at an early hour in the morning. A vast company gathered outside the church. The doors were suddenly thrown open. The empress, already crowned, looked small and timid but stately as she passed with slow and measured step to the royal carriage and drove to the Palace of Justice. She sat on her throne, quite still and silent, with magnificence all round her. At the great banquet which followed the soldiers feasted on raw meat. The carcase of a bullock was slung from a rope overhead and passed slowly along the table. Each man cut off the piece which pleased him best. It was a strange mixture of old ways and new.

The empress began her reign well. At her coronation she said that she was a small woman like Queen Victoria of England and like her she hoped to be a great woman. But all through Abyssinia, as at the banquet, old ways and new ways were in sharp contrast. The country was awaking. A desire for education and progress was stirring the younger men. In particular, the heir to the throne, Ras Tafari, the grand-nephew of Menelik II, was always in favour of advance. The empress took the other side. She wanted old ways and opposed new ones, as women in Africa and elsewhere have so often done. She tried to hold back the people. She stirred her husband to fight. But his soldiers were defeated by the party of progress. At that moment it was announced that the Empress Zauditu had died.

CHAPTER 2

AFRICAN QUEENS AND WOMAN CHIEFS

BESIDES the royal women of Egypt and Abyssinia many women of Negro or Bantu race have held rule in' Africa. The Queen Mothers, especially in Ashanti, have been storehouses of ancient custom and have also had large influence in the councils of the king. Some of them are very beautiful, as the first picture in this book shows. Leading African women often liked to show how independent they were. In the earlier part of the nineteenth century, for example, DOKUWA, queen of Akim, knew how to express her mind. The Ashantis and the British were at war. Each party sought to win the aid of Dokuwa's army, for her country lay on their line of march. She decided to fight for the British, but when she came in to tell them this she brought a live parrot on a pole. This was to show that as the parrot could fly off and hide in the forest so she could withdraw from her agreement if she liked.

The stories in this chapter are mostly from the past, but in many African districts women rulers are still to be found. When a leading chief in Tanganyika died recently his sister was named as his successor. The story of a Transvaal tribe which has a woman chief appeared in *The Times*, the best-known London newspaper, while this

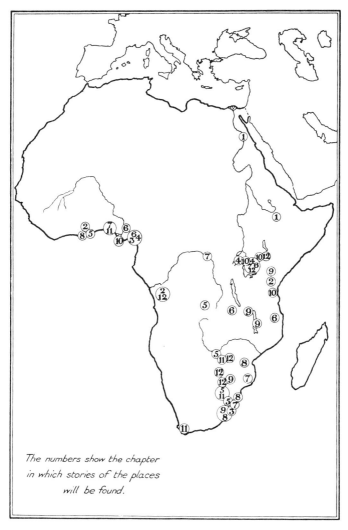

The numbers show the chapter
in which stories of the places
will be found.

MAP OF AFRICA

chapter was being written. She has great power
and all her people obey her. She has two head-
men to help her ; one deals with the affairs of the
tribe, the other with religious questions. The
queen has a husband but he holds no office, and
no one mentions his name. A recent traveller in
East Africa found four African judges trying a
case in the central Native Court. One of them
was a young woman in gay cotton clothing, who
took her full part in discussing the case. He
found it was the custom to put women on the
Councils of the Elders ; one whole district was
under the control of an efficient woman chief.

I

A QUEEN IN THE WEST

When Livingstone had nearly completed his
great journey right across Africa he arrived at a
Portuguese fort in Congoland. There, on a great
rock, the print of a woman's foot had been carved.
The people told him it was the footprint of the
great QUEEN NZINGA who had lived some three
hundred years before. Her full history can only
be found in curious old books.

King John II of Portugal had begun to send his
ships to the Congo coast, which afterwards became
a Portuguese colony. His missionaries made their
way inland and some of the Congo rulers and
many of the people became Christians. One of
the Congo kings was such a tyrant that his people
removed him from the throne. He left three
daughters, of whom Nzinga was one, and two
sons. One of the sons killed the other, then he

killed his sister Nzinga's son, and seized the throne. He began to quarrel with the Portuguese, but when a new governor came the Congo king thought there was a chance of making peace. It was not easy to do so, for the Portuguese were proud and strong. Who should go to make terms with them? The young king chose well. He sent his sister, the Princess Nzinga.

The Portuguese governor was amazed by the quick wit and power of the girl. He offered to make peace if the king would pay a tribute year by year. "People talk of tribute after they have conquered, not before it," replied Nzinga proudly. "We come to talk of peace, not of subjection." She won from the governor all that she desired. Before she returned to her brother from Loanda, where the governor was, she professed to be a Christian. But, as we shall see, Nzinga's new religion did not go very deep.

On reaching home, she persuaded her brother to ask for a Christian priest to teach his people. Very wisely the Portuguese sent him an African, one of his own subjects. But the king, taking this as an insult, treated the priest rudely and attacked the Portuguese. He was beaten three times, his followers deserted him, he fled to an island in the river, and there he died. Nzinga is believed to have poisoned him in revenge for his murder of her son.

Christianity did not fit in with such doings, so Nzinga gave it up. She ascended the throne, using all the bloodthirsty rites of former years when she was crowned. She began her reign by killing all whom she thought were her enemies. Then she declared war on Portugal. Once more she proudly refused to pay tribute as the price of peace. The Portuguese forces approached her camp on an island. She consulted the soothsayer who was in charge of her brother's spirit. He advised her not to face a battle, so Nzinga fled. The Portuguese pressed her hard. Her sisters were captured, but she escaped into a neighbouring kingdom. When the Portuguese withdrew Queen Nzinga returned, got another tribe to help her, and conquered the ancient kingdom of Matemba. She took the old queen and her daughter prisoners. The old queen was branded as a slave and died of grief, but the daughter was taken into favour. More conflicts followed with the Portuguese. Then peaceable relations were established for a time.

An old writer, who lived not long after Nzinga's day, gives a picture of this restless queen :

" She was a woman of judgment and so fond of fighting that she always dressed like a man and took hardly any exercise but that of a soldier. Yet she was so generous that she never suffered a Portuguese to be hurt after he had yielded on the battle field. She and her people for the most part led an unsettled life, roaming up and down. Before any enterprise was undertaken they asked counsel of the devil by sacrificing the wisest and most comely person they could pick out. On the occasion of this human sacrifice the Queen appeared with the skins of beasts hanging round her neck before and behind, a sword about her, an axe in her girdle, a bow and arrows in her hand. She leaped, according to their custom, now here, now there, as nimbly as the most active of her attendants ; all the while she struck two iron bells which served instead of drums. When she had wearied herself in this manner she took a broad feather and stuck it through her bored nose as a sign she was ready for war."

The treasure Nzinga most esteemed was a silver chest given her by the Portuguese in which she always carried her brother's bones. A few years later she again took to war. Wishing to capture a place where the Portuguese were, she sought for a favourable omen. She set a black cock and a white cock to fight with one another. When the black cock won, Nzinga made sure that her dark-faced army would succeed. But alas ! she was severely defeated and gave the Portuguese no more trouble for years.

The fierce old queen's conscience began at last to work. Some one brought her a crucifix which was said to have miraculous powers. She consulted the spirits of five of her ancestors. She believed they told her they were all in torment and that she would join them soon. They advised her to embrace the Christian faith again and make friends with the Portuguese.

There is a story in one of the old, old books of a meeting between the queen and a Portuguese Christian preacher at this time. He, wise man, praised the beauty of her valleys and pleasant streams sheltered by mountains. He asked, " Who is the author of all this ? Who made the ground fertile and ripened the corn ? " The queen stoutly replied, " My ancestors." The preacher asked if the power of her ancestors was also hers. " Yes," she answered, " and much more, for I am absolute mistress of Matemba." The preacher picked up a straw from the ground and said, " O Queen, do me the favour to cause this straw to hang in the air without holding it." The queen turned away with scorn from so small a request. But the preacher urged it. So she tried. The straw fell to the ground. "It fell," he said, "because you did not command it to hang in the air." At last the queen gave the order but the straw did not obey. Then the Portuguese preacher spoke. "Be it known to your majesty, O Queen, that your ancestors were no more able to produce these fair fields and springs than you are able by your command to support this straw." At last, as he told her of the great Creator who was the cause of all things, she was convinced. She professed to be a Christian once more. Not long after she died.

II

ON THE SLOPES OF A SNOW-CROWNED MOUNTAIN

1. *The Story of Queen Mashina*

Right across Africa on the slopes of the snow-crowned mountain Kilimanjaro; many fine women have claimed a place in the history of their country. Among them are two whose stories are told here. Their names are MASHINA and NUYA.

Long years ago, a chief of the little state of Mamba married the daughter of a chief who lived near by. She brought with her a young servant named Mashina. After a time the wife's father became jealous and persuaded his daughter to poison her husband. Mashina discovered the plot.

She warned her master and saved his life. He was so grateful that he married her. When he died the people chose Mashina to succeed him and loved her more than any of their former chiefs.

Two African friends, one a descendant of the clan of Mashina, the other a teacher in Mamba, have written for us in their own language the story of Mashina's life and death. A missionary who lives in Mashina's country has translated it into English. Here it is :

" Mashina governed her country well. She opened a market for the selling of cattle in order that the poor people might be able to buy them. She also was liberal, for she gave an order that a cow or perhaps a goat should be given to any poor person who brought to her two banana plants, or two loads of grass or one load of banana leaves. When a child was born in your house and you went to the chief and told her, ' Chief, I have been given a child,' she would present you with a cow and a goat and tell you to take them home. She made the country richer by making the people till the ground so that it produced fruit.

" Mashina's love was great. She ordered that all small children who lost their father and mother should be brought to her, that she might take care of them. There were so many children in her house that they had to sleep in the little store-hut for the beer corn because there was no other room. She also loved the women of her country, especially the widows. When she killed cattle to distribute among her people she gave strict orders that widows should have their portion of meat.

" Mashina also loved war and enriched her country by bringing back great booty and many cattle, to the astonishment of all. She accomplished this through boldness and strict discipline. She learned war like a man, and carried a man's weapons—the double-edged sword, the spear, and the shield. After her death the country slid back into its former laziness and the people no more tilled the ground. Then her enemies the Wapare, whom she had conquered, composed a song, ' Mashina has died ; let us pasture our cattle in the plains again, where there is grass, because there will be no more war but freedom.'

" The story of Mashina's murder is this. She ordered some work to be done by everybody. One man named Nyapo Tembo did not go. Mashina punished him for his disobedience. He was angry and went away with his wife in the night to a place called Kilema. He asked the people, ' Where is the chief ? ' They told him, ' He is at home.' The chief was called and came to meet Nyapo and his wife in the courtyard of the judgment hall. The chief asked, ' Where do you come from, my son ? ' Nyapo answered, ' I come from Mamba, chief, where I have been robbed of my only cow. Therefore I have moved away and ask you to give me a place.' The chief ordered a man to be driven away from his lot that the stranger might have a dwelling-place. He and his wife were given land and also a cow which was in calf.

" Then Nyapo implored the chief of Kilema, who was called Rangoma, saying : ' Now give me eight men that I may go to Mamba and kill the chief. When I have succeeded in killing her, her people will be scattered and the power of Mashina's country will be broken.' Rangoma hated Mashina and agreed to do this.

" Nyapo set out to Mamba with his eight men, carrying spears. They took up a position on the hill where the Christian church now stands. When the people of Mamba saw them they shouted for help. Mashina, thinking that her cattle kraal on the hill was in danger, went up with a few men. Nyapo and his followers hid among the crops and waylaid the chief. They sprang out like leopards and killed one of her party with spears. Then they returned to Kilema singing, ' We have killed Mawindi ! We have killed Mawindi ! ' Mawindi was a headman of the chief and was famous for courage. But Mashina herself was not hurt.

" Well, when Mawindi had died, Chief Rangoma of Kilema built a bridge across the River Wona which divides Mamba from Kilema. He came from Kilema to Mamba with all his people to call on Chief Mashina. Having paid his visit he went home. Another day he came again and spoke to Mashina thus : ' Why ! Am I to come to you every day to call on you, but you don't come to pay me a visit even once ? Well, let us go together to Kilema to-day.' Mashina consented and went. Rangoma gave her a house to sleep in near Nyangu, the hill near the place where the mission now is. Mashina stayed there but Rangoma made a plot. He sent people to offer Mashina the services of a little girl who was to sleep with her. Those men told the little girl that she must do everything they told her. When she promised to obey their orders, they continued :

" ' We shall come in the night with a rope when Chief Mashina is asleep, and make a hole in the hut where she puts her head. We shall pass in the rope with a noose. You will receive it and lay

it round her neck gently while she is sleeping.
Then we shall pull outside.'

" Well, they carried out their plan. They came
in the night with the rope, gave it to the girl, who
received it and put it round Mashina's neck, and
those outside pulled till she was dead.

" Then Chief Kilema divided Mashina's land
with another chief. And they carried off all the
riches of Mashina and of the people of Mamba."

2. *The Story of Mother Nuya*

Here is the story of Nuya. She was wife of the
chief of Machame, the largest chieftainship of
Kilimanjaro. Her husband died, leaving his son
Shangali, a mere boy, to succeed him. A young
chief named Sima, who had been sheltered and
protected by Nuya's husband years before when

MOTHER NUYA SEEKING PEACE

he was in distress, resolved to try to seize Machame for himself. He threatened the country with war. The new Machame chief was too young to lead his men to battle. But the boy had a mother, and Nuya was worth more than an army to her son.

One day a strange little party set off through the forest. It consisted of Nuya herself, with an elder of the tribe, a boy, and a young girl leading a lamb to show that they were seeking peace. Right up to the enemy's army she went and boldly demanded to see Sima, the chief. He was now a fierce and bloodthirsty warrior who was never known to turn aside from war. But Nuya, with her lamb, made her way into his presence and reminded him of what her husband had done for him in past years. She asked him in gratitude to lay down his arms. Sima yielded and made peace.

Nuya was the strength and counsellor of her son Shangali through many troubled years. The seat of authority was sometimes hers. After years of being ruler Shangali felt the burden of work too heavy, so he ordered his young son, Abdieli, to return from school and help him. Hearing that the story of Nuya was to be told in this book, M.H. Abdieli wrote down in Swaheli his grandmother's life. We thank him very much. It is translated into English by the German missionary who sent also the story of Mashina.

" On the fifth of May, 1930," writes the young chief, " Chief Shangali enthroned his son Abdieli to be chief of Machame in the presence of the government representative and more than 8,000 elders and men of the tribe. Mother Nuya and Chief Shangali handed over the seat of authority in the presence of all the people. Mother Nuya

seized the right hand of her grandson and Chief
Shangali his left and seated M.H. Abdieli upon the
seat of authority. They handed it over to him
and the people shouted ' Hurrah ' three times.
Since that day M.H. Abdieli has taken on him the
name of chief and Mother Nuya is living with him,
as is the· custom of the Wachaga, that she may
teach him the ways of the country. She is
helped by the elders of the country and his father,
Shangali.

" Mother Nuya is now a woman of eighty-eight
years of age. But she still has strength enough to
walk about and do her work. Since she saw that
all her grandchildren have been baptised in the
Christian faith, urged by the power of God, Mother
Nuya agreed to become a Christian in 1930.
Mother Nuya has begun to attend the instructions.

" Mother Nuya is much honoured here at
Machame because she is a kind and merciful
mother. Again she is a very clever mother, for she
knows many laws of the country of the Wachaga.
Though she is a very old mother her power of
reasoning and her character have not yet begun
to change. With about half her property she has
helped to educate poor children without being
paid anything. She does this still. Whenever
she knows any person to be quarrelling with his
neighbour or brother and to be causing enmity,
Mother Nuya tries very hard to persuade them to
come to an agreement and to live at peace. She
even suffers loss of property because of these
attempts. Therefore there are many people who
love to honour her much."

The wife of the government officer who was
present when Chief Abdieli was enthroned knew

Mother Nuya years ago and loved her.   She wrote these words in a book :

" Nuya may be seen passing among the elders and youths of the district, who silently step aside and watch her with loving attention.   She is now a great-grandmother and though somewhat stout bears herself with queenly dignity and grace.   Her few quiet words are listened to with close attention by her followers.   The flashing light in her clear brown eyes reveals a keen mind and a youthful spirit.   She is an example of what the best of her sex can show in Africa."

CHAPTER 3

IN THE HEART OF TRIBAL AFRICA

I

FAMOUS WOMEN IN ZULULAND

IN olden days in Zululand 'there were women whose stories are still told. Some of them lived to a great age. The grandmother of Chaka—his father's mother—only died in 1825. She was then about ninety-five years of age and thousands mourned at her funeral. She had three daughters ; the two eldest, who were twins, never married, but became heads of kraals. One was a strong and rather fierce woman who cared for her young brother's kingdom till he was old enough to rule. She held high rank and was looked up to with respect. She was a friend of Chaka's mother, Nandi, but in later years became a bitter enemy of Chaka himself. She and her twin sister stirred up his younger brothers to kill him.

The third daughter of Chaka's grandmother, named MAWA, married and bore a son. She then retired to rule over a royal kraal. But evil omens disturbed her. A crow perched on a fence and foretold the destruction of her people. So Mawa gathered up her goods and left. She arrived with a following at the Tukela River. White soldiers from Cape Town stopped her advance. So she settled down in grass tents where she was. Later on a bad drought in Zululand brought many people to join her party. Mawa became a little queen again. Her grave lies on a small rocky hill amid fields of green sugar-cane.

We know from Chaka's story that his father had many wives. Some of them were remarkable women. The great wife lived on long after her husband's death. She was protected in turn by Chaka and his brothers who were chiefs after him. Cetshwayo, the well-known Zulu chief, cared for her after Chaka's brothers died until he was himself defeated. Then she took her own life. Another wife of Chaka's father lived through the reign of five Zulu chiefs.

But NANDI, Chaka's mother, was the best known of all the wives. Her love for the man she chose, the early birth of Chaka, her son, the indignation of the other wives, and her final banishment by her husband, make one of the great stories of Zululand. A beautiful picture of loyal motherhood is given in her devotion to Chaka through his stormy boyhood, her steady effort to influence him and check his thirst for blood, and her vain plea that he would marry and leave a son to succeed him. Chaka loved no other as he loved her. He went straight to ruin after Nandi's death.

A fine story is told about NOWAWA, the mother of Zwide, a chief who was a determined enemy of Chaka. Zwide's pride had been hurt because another chief, the head of the Ngoni tribe, had been generous to him and set him free after conquering him. Instead of being grateful for this mercy Zwide resolved to destroy the chief and his tribe. The old story as the Africans tell it goes something like this :

" Zwide's mother reasoned with him saying, ' My child, shall the Ngoni perish ? Did they not send you back after taking you captive, giving you many fat cattle to bring with you ? Is it right to go out to war against them ? ' But Zwide gave no heed to his mother's words and called his soldiers together. On the day when they were being reviewed before battle, the mother of Zwide planned to make the soldiers afraid. She went into the cattle fold (no woman was ever allowed there) where the soldiers were. Standing in their midst she began to take off her clothes. The soldiers, seeing this, greatly wondered. Zwide was startled too. The soldiers began to think it was an omen ; perhaps the spirits of the ancestors had told her to do this strange thing. They lost courage, and being afraid to go to battle were disbanded. So Nowawa, Zwide's mother, prevailed."

II

THE STORY OF A WOMEN'S RISING

Some years ago, in a province of Southern Nigeria, a white woman was busy in her little house not far from the road. She heard the sound of numberless feet. She went to the door and stood amazed. There, along the road at the end of her garden, a great company of women was tramping past. Each held a short stick in her hand. Grave, silent, determined, they looked neither to the right nor to the left. Something

BUNDU WOMEN ON THE MARCH—A WOMEN'S SECRET SOCIETY IN SIERRA LEONE

(The two central figures are Bundu "devils," supposed to be spirits in human form.)

held them together; they had a common end in
view.

One of them stopped for a moment. The white
woman asked her courteously whither she and her
friends were going and whence they came. A
brief answer was given. The woman hastened on.
The party swept out of sight.

It appeared that the marching women belonged
to a local branch of one of the women's secret
societies of West Africa. A member of the society
had broken one of the rules which happened also
to be a law of the land. The case was being tried
at the Native Court. The women's society was
going in a body to see that justice was done and
the offender was punished. In the evening the
party tramped back again, silent, vexed, and tired.
There had not been time in court to try the case
that day. It was put off to the following meeting.

On the next court day the same body of women
marched past, resolute as before. In the evening
their return was made known by gay laughter and
talk. The case had been heard. The verdict
they desired had been given. The honour of
their society was saved.

The missionary knew about the secret societies
to which no man might belong. She had heard
of their solemn meetings and of their curious
dresses and rites. But now she realised, more
than ever before, how strong the African tribal
women could be when they stood together. She
saw the force of their united will, whether used for
evil or for good.

Towards the close of the year 1929 there was a
remarkable rising of women in the province of Old
Calabar and Owerri in Southern Nigeria. When

it was over the Government appointed a commission of six important men to make inquiries as to the cause of the rising, and what happened when the women were in revolt. The report of this Commission is printed in a large book. With it is a much larger book—really a huge one—containing every question which the witnesses were asked and every answer which they gave. Many of the witnesses were African women. Copies of the two big books can be seen in London ; I have just been reading in them some things the African women said.

What was the cause of the rising ? There were some old grounds for discontent in the women's minds. But the new and most serious one was really all a mistake. Instructions had been given by the authorities that the people and their possessions were to be counted ; the women were to be counted with the rest. Some time before the men had been counted and then they had been taxed. Now, as the women were going to be counted, some one started the idea that the women were about to be taxed like the men. This seemed dreadful to these tribal women. They felt they helped to earn some of the money which paid the taxes of the men. They certainly were not willing to pay taxes themselves. They did not know that in England and other countries women often pay taxes as well as men.

As a matter of fact, the authorities had no idea of taxing the women. When the trouble began the officials were slow to realise what it was about. The women were ignorant and very suspicious. When the officials denied that women were going to be taxed the women refused to believe them.

Wild stories went round, bad rumours spread from place to place. Every effort made to show the women that they were mistaken failed. They really believed that the tax would come upon them if they did not resist with all their might.

Some people said the men of the tribes were behind the women, urging them on. But this was not the case. As one of the women leaders said, " We were not encouraged by the men. It is not true. We acted according to our consciences. The matter did not concern men."

A great deal of trouble was given and much harm was done. Great masses of women gathered under women leaders who were able to control and direct them. Buildings were attacked and wrecked. Offices and banks were raided. Order was badly disturbed. Crowds refused to break up. Lives were in danger. Police and soldiers were called in. Several times fire-arms had to be used and some women lost their lives. At one place a missionary doctor was able to control a crowd of women by getting two hundred patients from a leper home to make a guard. Very, very slowly the women learned that they had been mistaken. At last they believed the statements made to them and went home.

After the rising was over the Commissioners began their work. They pointed out that the counting was begun in a way which alarmed the women. They suggested how future misunderstandings might be avoided. Of course the Commissioners saw how suspicious and unreasonable the women had been, but they saw something else as well. They said the women who had caused the trouble were worth having as friends.

They thought that the Ibo˙ and Ibibio women —
those were the two leading tribes in the rising—
showed capacity for organisation and leadership.
They asked that the influence of the women might
be recognised. They wrote some generous words
about the African women who gave evidence before
them. Here is what the six men on the Government Commission said :

" No one listening to the evidence given before
us could have failed to be impressed by the intelligence, the power of exposition, the directness and
the mother-wit some of the leaders showed. . . .
The lessons learned from their demonstrations
should be taken to heart."

III

Mbafo and Mboro

There was no darker spot in all West Africa
than the shrine of the Long Ju-ju at Arochuku in
Calabar. It was the centre for human sacrifices
and for slave trade. So dark and evil were the
deeds, so cruel the burden laid upon the people,
that a British military expedition was sent up to
rid the country of the scourge. The stream that
ran through the Ju-ju grove, often red with the
blood of sacrifices, now flows peacefully through
banks set with growing corn. It supplies pure
and wholesome water to a splendid training home
for African girls.

Here is the story of Nue-Nue Mbafo. In the
old days of the Long Ju-ju, she was the wife of
the chief who had most to do with the slave trade
round the horrible spot. She was foremost among

the women, leading in their dances and taking chief part in their sacrifices.   In the secret societies of the women she was a leader too.

Her husband was a chief of influence and wealth. Just before the Aro expedition he went down to Calabar to collect money due to him for slaves. Being known as an Aro of high position he was held a prisoner there.   The news of this dismayed his people in Aro.   They consulted their witch doctors and magicians.   Big sums of money were offered to Chuku and other gods.   In all this Mbafo as chief wife took first place.   It was of no avail.

Mbafo sacrificed day by day everything that was suggested—fowls, goats, dogs.   She walked from one magician to another, paying them whatever they asked.   Nothing happened.   Night after night she spent in the compound pacing to and fro, hoping her husband might come.   He never came.

Some time before, an African trader had come up from Bonny and tried to tell the Aro about God. Mbafo had led the opposition against him.   Now, in her despair, she remembered what he had said. One starry night she wandered in the bush in great agony of soul.   One star, bigger and brighter than the rest, hung in the sky.   Perhaps behind that star there was a Power who could help her; it might be this new God.   She stood still with up-turned face and outstretched arms and cried aloud :

" God, Great God, I know not what you are.   I know not where you are.   But if you can hear, listen to my sorrow.   If you can see, look on me in pity.   God, Great God, I know not, I know not."

Two days later her husband came home. Now Calabar is two days' journey from Aro. He must have started just after her prayer. There was rejoicing and feasting. As Mbafo told the chief the story of the star he started in amazement. He knew about the Power, he said. Some one he met in Calabar told him about " the white man's God " who heard and answered when men called.

Some years later the chief became a member of the Christian Church. This meant giving up his many wives and making provision for them. He would have chosen Mbafo as his " church wife," but she refused. He must take a younger woman. She said this partly for his sake, partly because if she was outcast herself she could help the other outcast women.

Mbafo was the first Aro woman to become a member of the Christian Church. This was in 1910. She was also the first Aro woman to go against public opinion and save the life of twins. Sometimes her house was full of babies and their mothers. Before she grew too old and weak to carry on this work she had saved many twins and their mothers. No matter how ill she was, the news that twins had been born restored her vigour. She was up and off and never rested till she had the babies safely in her house.

At last she was no longer able for the task, so other Christian women built a compound just for twins and their mothers. They did part of the building themselves and raised money to pay for the rest. The compound has eight houses and is meant for twins born in towns where there is no Christian influence. In towns where a church has been formed the women members make it their special work to protect the twins and their mothers. There are about forty twins now in these Aro towns under ten years old. Their presence is slowly but surely driving away the superstitious fear of twin babies which is deeply felt in many African tribes. That is the story of Mbafo. The story of Mboro comes next.

In every Aro town it has been the custom to employ a woman to kill twins as soon as they are born, in order to save the town from misfortune. One of these women was named MBORO. While she was out on the farm one day she became the grandmother of twins. There was the usual commotion in the place. The indignant grandmother hastened home to do her work of killing the babies, but some of the Christian women and a white missionary arrived first. The grandmother could not get into the house. She cursed and stormed and threatened. She would act when the white woman had gone. But watch was kept night and day. The twins prospered because the mother was protected and could care for them.

Meantime the old grandmother was not happy at all. There was life and joy in the house and she had no share in it. She began to think. One day she was seen peering in at the door. She watched the twins but did not enter. Next day she peeped in again. A Christian who was taking charge held one of the babies towards her. The old woman was conquered, she took the baby in her arms.

From that day her interest grew. Soon she told the missionary there was no need to watch over the twins, she would care for them herself. And she did. Never were twin babies better cared for. Six months later wails of distress from the next compound told that twins had been born there too. The grandmother from next door rushed in, not to kill but to save. " More twins ? " she exclaimed ; " bring them to my house beside our twins and I will care for them." So mother and babies came along. A month later twins were born in another house. Again the grandmother offered them a home. There was no prouder woman in all Arochuku than old Mboro, with her six twins and three mothers of twins to care for and protect.

CHAPTER 4

THE ARO MIDWIFE AND THE TORO WITCH

I

ADA, THE ARO MIDWIFE

ADA was a friend of Mbafo and like many other women of the Aro tribe she had an active and interesting life. She was always a leader among the women. She was perhaps the most popular midwife, surgeon, and doctor in the whole district. She did the various cuttings of tribal marks for children and girls.

Ada was a woman of middle size, active and vigorous. She moved so quickly that there was always a flutter when she passed. She shouted her greetings in her hearty way as she hastened along the path. The slower, duller people stood by the wayside and turned to shout their greetings after her, for she had gone by before they could speak.

The story of how Ada became a Christian is one of those strange tales which one can repeat but cannot explain. There were some of Ada's friends among the first Aro who were baptised. Ada kept away from them, but they always watched to do any kindness for their former friend. One day she was taken suddenly and violently ill. They

came to visit her and tried to help. But she got
steadily worse. After a night of great agony she
" died " in the early morning. That is the story
as Ada and her friends always told it themselves.

The household began to wail. The relatives
started to dig the grave. The Christian women,
led by Mbafo, were inspired with a great idea.
Four of them went into the little dark room where
the body lay and shut the door. All day long they
continued to pray that Ada might be restored to
them. Outside the door preparations were being
made for the burial. After the usual custom,
companies of people came to wail. Then the
relatives clamoured for the body to bury it. But
the four women would not open the door. At
sunset Ada opened her eyes and sat up.

The news was passed outside. A mighty fear
fell upon the people. They rushed out of the
compound. The praying women brought Ada
food and water.

In a short time Ada regained her former vigour.
But she was a changed woman. She sought only
the company of the Christians and after a time
became one herself. All her old powers of leadership brought her to the front. At first she gave up
all her medical practices as " heathen " things.
But wise white friends pointed out to her that her
knowledge of herbs and roots was a valuable gift
and ought to be used for the healing of sick folk.
As soon as she was assured of this she became
again the midwife and surgeon, not now for cutting
tribal marks, but for the treatment of abscesses and
other swellings. One day she collected before her
house all the ju-jus and charms she had used, and

in the presence of the Church people she destroyed by fire every evil thing she had possessed.

Then she became a friend to women when their babies were born. Heathen and Christian alike felt safer when Ada was at hand. She insisted, and quietly gained her point, that no ju-ju or charm should come near her patients. She learned from her missionary friend the value of cleanliness and care in her cases. She became a health visitor of great use. Her patients must often have thought that she was mad when she did things contrary to custom. But they feared and respected her too much not to obey. The babies that Ada brought into the world lived and grew strong.

About seven years ago Ada died. After her death the compound was crowded but there was no loud wailing. Her Christian friends numbered many hundreds and followed her coffin to church. The heathen people she loved, and who loved her, remained by the house rocking themselves to and fro and crying quietly. The women, old and grey-haired and young, were in heartfelt grief. Over and over again they said softly, " Ada our mother has left us. Who will help us now ? Ada our mother has gone. A-me-oh ! O pity us. Ada our mother has gone ; we have no one to help us now. A-me-oh ! Ada our mother has gone."

II

KAGEI, THE KING OF TORO'S WITCH

There are two people in this story—Kasagama, king of Toro, a country west of Uganda, and KAGEI, his witch. The story is in four parts.

KAGEI, ONCE THE KING OF TORO'S WITCH

The first part shows the witch dancing on the night of the new moon. The second part shows her travelling with the king and his company to Uganda. The third tells what came to Kagei in that country. The fourth shows her return to Toro and what she did.

I. All Toro drummed a greeting to the new moon that night, but the great gathering was on the hill-top by the house of the king. The six royal drummers worked with a will. Men and women with sweat pouring from them danced with more energy than joy. The king sat in state on a high native stool facing the moon. He watched closely the movements of a stately woman strangely dressed. Her face, though scarred by smallpox, was striking. Her eyes, black as night, seemed to flash out fire. She looked like a great woman in the tribe. As her body swayed to and fro in the dance she kept her eyes fixed upon the king. He was a tall, handsome man, light in colour, his features fine in shape. His silk cloth was wrapped loosely round him, he wore a white turban on his head.

The dance still continued, but suddenly the woman he was watching came to his side. " Times are not well with Toro," she said. Anxiously the two talked together, then, rising, they went to the king's private room. No one but Kagei could go there at any time unasked. Sitting on a lion skin beside his stool the witch told her story. The king's mind was filled with fear. Had not Kagei once saved him from smallpox by taking the disease on herself ? Was she not able to see evil before it came ? The king dare not brush her sense of danger aside.

II. Next morning preparations for a journey

were hastily made. For the first time a king of Toro was going to Uganda. And the all-powerful witch, Kagei, was going too. Rumour was busy in Toro. Was the king going to lay down his crown before Mwanga, king of Uganda ? Or was he going with Kagei to get the teachers who had brought the new Faith to Uganda turned out and all who had followed them destroyed ? So the people questioned, but the king and the witch held their peace. There was no need yet for the people to know that an old enemy, daring and strong, was threatening Toro once more. The great white Kapere,[1] who had driven him away before, was in Uganda still. Perhaps, if they asked him, he would give his aid again.

The king set out for Uganda, amid the rolling of the drums and the thronging of his people. He was carried in a huge basket attached to poles by some of his strongest subjects. Round his neck was the charm Kagei had given the previous evening to make his journey safe. It was a lion's claw covered with purple beads holding medicine. Behind him and his bearers came Kagei in a hammock with her attendants.

Walking quietly in the background, well out of Kagei's sight, was Rubeni, a man of Uganda. He had come to Toro to teach the new Faith. Kasagama liked to have him in the party because he knew Uganda ways. Gradually the crowd of followers thinned. Only a few crossed the frontier with the king and his witch. After ten days' journey they arrived at Mwanga's court.

III. Kasagama saw Kapere, who promised the help he asked. And Kapere, who saw what the

---

[1] Captain Lugard, now Lord Lugard.

new Faith was doing for Uganda, actually urged Kasagama to become a Christian too. Rubeni came often, and brought the chief of the white teachers to see the Toro king. Kasagama listened with open ears. One night he called on Kagei to tell her all he was learning and ask her to listen too. She was deeply disturbed. She secretly tried to hold Kasagama back. He feared her more than anyone on earth. But he would not let her hold him back. He made up his mind to be a Christian and was baptised in the great church of the capital of Uganda.

Poor Kagei, how lonely she was ! How she feared, sometimes for Toro, sometimes for herself. Would his people turn against Kasagama because of the message he had heard ? And now she felt that message making its way to her own heart. As a magician she had won great wealth ; could she bear to be poor ? The other magicians would want to kill her ; could she lay down her life as Jesus, the Lord of the new Faith, had done ? At last Kagei could wait no longer. She went and told the king. He was full of joy. He and Kagei had worked so long together. Now they would work in the new Faith.

IV. The party marched back to Toro. Each night in camp the king, Kagei, and Rubeni talked and talked. At last they reached the hill-top where the moonlight dance was held. Silence reigned as the king stood before his people. He wore a wonderful head-dress decorated with cowrie shells and the red tail-feathers of a parrot. Kagei stood by him, no longer muffled up like a magician but with uncovered head, her cloth draped to her shoulders.

In simple words the king told his people he had become a Christian. Then, laying his hand upon Kagei's shoulder, he went on : " I want to tell you that the great magician of my family wants to be a Christian too." The crowd cried out in excitement, " Kagei ? Kagei ? " A leading chief exclaimed, " Our king and our chief magician are deserting us ! What sorrow for the land ! "

Next morning the king met his council and told them he would build a church. Some chiefs were willing, but the most important of all was angry and would not agree. On Sunday the king with a great crowd went to Rubeni's little reed church. Kagei also was there. Suddenly, pushing rudely through the people, came the chief who was opposing the king. He had been drinking spirits. He stormed loudly with shameful words against the followers of Jesus Christ. Then a strange thing happened. Here is the story, told by one who knew Kagei well.

" The people were all filled with fear. Suddenly Kagei stood up, a majestic figure. With her piercing eye fixed upon the chief she pointed at the doorway. She spoke not a word, but her gaze and her attitude were full of meaning. The man stood speechless before her and silence fell upon the crowd. He tried to speak, then a look of fear came into his face and before Kagei's eyes he seemed to crumble into helplessness. Still she stood pointing to the door and in the silence one word came from her lips—' *Isoko !* ' (Go !). He was gone."

Kagei sat down. Rubeni went on with his service ; the people sang a hymn.

The king had a wise counsellor in Kagei, who

was still a power in the land. She led the women who helped to build the new white teacher's house. She learned to read. Rubeni taught her about the new religion. When the chief of all the white teachers came to visit Toro she was baptised.

Kagei was once the woman most feared in Toro, now she became the woman most loved. Children no longer ran to hide in the forest when she appeared. She taught the little princesses how to spin. She went first to teach the Faith to the women in the cow kraals in Ankole. Then she came back to Toro and was matron in the school for girls. She died in 1930.

This is the true story of Kagei, once king Kasagama's witch.

CHAPTER 5

CHANGING AFRICA

I

OPENING THE TREASURES OF THE EARTH

CHANGES are common to all lands. But in Africa a few years have brought as much change as centuries elsewhere. New things have come one on top of another with breathless speed. This is partly because life moves more quickly to-day than in the past. But the main reason is that tribal Africa, with its ancient ways, has rapidly been brought into touch with the most advanced nations of the world.

"NEW THINGS COME WITH BREATHLESS SPEED"

In past centuries ships crept round the coast-line and bold explorers pushed in here and there. Now the whole of Africa has been opened up. New railways and motor roads are being made every year. Harbours are being improved. The number of lake and river steamboats increases. Great airways begin to cross Africa. The slow toil of the caravan, the weary march of the long lines of porters is almost over. There is scarcely a corner of Africa which the white man has not seen, or a tribe so remote as to have had no dealings with him.

Livingstone believed that the only way to check the slave trade in Africa was to open up honest trade. To-day, up all the ways newly opened into the heart of Africa traders bring goods from other lands. Distant kraals and villages are supplied with things made across the seas. And down the same rail and road and waterways African products pass out into the world. All this has worked some evil as well as good.

The discovery of mineral wealth in Africa has brought more sweeping changes to pass than has trade. Wherever great stores of coal, or tin, or copper, or gold-bearing ore have been found African labour has been required. Recruiting agents have gone out far and near to enlist men for the work. The pay offered at the mines tempts those who are short of money with which to pay their taxes, or who are in debt, or who want to pay *lobolo* for a wife.

From districts anywhere south of the Zambesi the great call is to the Johannesburg mines. Thousands of young men make the long trek away from their homes and their people. Will they ever come back to them and to the old simple ways of life ? After a medical examination they are passed into the mine compound, bound until their contract has expired. Then they can go home again, or sign on for another term in the mine, or go out to seek for work in the city.

In the best mines an attempt is made to care properly for the men. But the work is hard and at best unhealthy. Men in the vigour of life often fall victims to accident and disease. In the unnatural conditions of the mining compound perils beset young men cut off from their families. Vices which haunt the compounds ruin many. But some make a splendid stand and return home stronger than before. A visitor noticed a white paper on the door of a mine compound one day. On it he found, in three African languages, these words—" Blessed are the pure in heart for they shall see God." It had been put up by a group of young Christian tribesmen working in the mine.

When a recruit has finished his contract he may decide to stay on in Johannesburg and look for work. Perhaps he has sent money home to his wife and family ; or saved his earnings hoping to use them to profit. Or he may have forgotten those he left behind him and have wasted all he earned.

In the great city—the second largest in Africa— he finds himself one of a vast multitude adrift from their father's ways. They have become " town Natives." As a rule they serve the white people engaged in business, and do the rougher work of the city. Locations are set apart for them and these are being gradually improved. Here and there a real little home may be found. Outside the locations people are either scattered in quarters provided by their employers or are crowded together in "yards," some of which are still miserable and insanitary places lacking the decencies of home, where drink and vice flourish unchecked.

The number of African girls and women who share these conditions increases every year. Some flock to the towns in search of change and amusement. Some come to rejoin husbands who have sent for them or to seek husbands who have left them forsaken at home. Others dream that in the city work can be had for the asking, with good conditions and high pay. They soon discover their mistake.

Opening the treasures of the earth in Africa has brought fresh problems to many human lives.

II

OPENING THE TREASURES OF THE MIND

A greater change has come to the African people through the opened door of knowledge, a new cultivation of their mind. It is worth more to Africa and to the world than pathways of trade, mines of copper, or reefs of gold-bearing ore, for people are always worth more than things. Slowly but surely the education which has transformed the West is making its way through Africa. It starts in little bush schools and stretches upward and onward through schools of every grade. It begins with boys and men, but girls and women are included more and more. Only the ignorant cling to the old idea that African women are slow and stupid and cannot learn as easily as African men. Education brings the African into the common life of the world. It has begun to equip him—and her—for many forms of responsible work. It is calling out native gift for art and music. It is giving young Africans a literature which their own civilization has failed to provide, and giving scope for their literary powers. This book bears witness on page after page to the treasure which is revealed when fresh light is let into the African mind and brings new truths to enrich their ancient store.

But there has come to Africa a still greater treasure of the mind than even education itself. One Sunday afternoon, some six years ago, a well-known African of Zulu race stood in Hyde Park in London. He listened for some time to an atheist preacher proclaiming to a group of people his barren creed—" There is no God." Quietly the African turned away. " No one in my country," he said, " would listen to *that*." He was right. Africa even in its darkest days had, as Dr. Aggrey loved to point out, a wonderful sense of the Unseen. Religion is part of the African's nature ; without it he cannot live.

To ancient African beliefs the Arab, when he came, added the great faith of Islam. The African, hitherto bookless, had now a sacred book. In certain areas Islam became his religion ; in others he blended it with his old beliefs.

But when the new day began to dawn it brought to Africa a religion full of power. The Christian faith, once at home on its northern shores, came back to Africa. It began at once to make Africans new men and women. It has only begun its work. It is the most hidden and the most persistent of all the great forces working in the land. It has done much for men ; for women it has done even more. One of the greatest gifts which education and religion have jointly brought to Africa is the Christian Bible, now the most widely read book in the continent, whether in English or in the African languages.

African men who desire to understand what worthy womanhood is like will do well to study that book. Women step out from the pages wonderfully like some of Africa's best. Others rise up into heights of pure wifehood and mother-hood far above the level of to-day.

The most beautiful pictures of women in the Bible are those of two simple village maidens, one in the earlier, the other in the later books. One is Ruth, who worked in the cornfields, loyal and loving, full of grace and sweetness. She married the landowner Boaz and is the only woman whose name is mentioned in the long lists of those who were counted as ancestors of Jesus Christ. The other lovely picture, hundreds of years later, is that of Mary, the Mother of Jesus Christ. The beauty of her character and the wonder of her story have inspired artists in every age. Among the noble and touching stories of women in every land her figure stands out, the most favoured among all women, the perfect type of pure and self-sacrificing motherhood.

III

GAIN AND LOSS IN WOMEN'S LIVES

What has all this change brought to the African woman ? She has gained by education, by friendship with many fine women from the West, and by the coming of a religion which can make her pure and free, and open to her pathways of service. Much of her old bondage to custom and heavy labour is being removed. Nevertheless the woman shares in the loss as well as the gain. Few people realise how deeply the movement to the towns affects the life of the African woman, both those who go there and those who stay at home.

The women who go with their husbands, or follow them, exchange familiar work for conditions strange and unknown. The young wife and mother had in the village a position and possibly a little money of her own. No one interfered with the duties which were clearly hers. She had a fixed share in cultivating the garden, she marketed the produce, she fed the family. Transplant her to town and everything is changed. She lives in small quarters, shared perhaps with another family. She has no standing of her own. The things she did successfully are all out of reach. If she seeks work, she may, at best, take in washing for a white family ; at worst, she may take to brewing Kafir beer, which is against the law. Many temptations press round her ; she may easily slip into evil and vicious ways. Nevertheless there are women from the country who have managed to make true homes in a great city. All honour is due to them.

Tests just as grave come to the wife left in the village when the husband goes off for long periods of work. In some of the villages in Matabeleland, for instance, there are hundreds of women who do all the ploughing, planting, cultivating, and harvesting. They tend the cattle, sheep, and goats. They maintain their children, send them to school, and look after the family interests when the village council meets. The husbands may come home

TAKING IN WASHING—JOHANNESBURG

once a month ; or once a year (in October) for the ploughing ; or not for two years. They may send home money, or send goods such as ploughs, bedsteads, sewing machines, blankets ; or they may send nothing at all. The women often bear the whole burden without help. A capable woman has been known to handle money and family affairs so wisely that her husband returned to a well-built village, good grain lands, a herd of cattle, and a position of some importance.

The sorrow and loss which come to many women through their husband's absence is seen in such stories as these.

BUNJELU'S husband left her about twelve years ago and went to look for work. He wrote a few times in the first year. Then he wrote no more. His wife heard he was in prison, charged with stealing a bag of maize. Then he disappeared and has not been heard of for eight years. Bunjelu toiled away on the land, using her little stock of cows and sheep and goats to support her five children. When one boy was educated he helped to send the next brother to school. Bunjelu was bitter about her absent husband and weary under the load of work. At last, though she belonged to a Christian church, she agreed to be the wife of a polygamist. But he tired of her and she returned humbly to her own little village and started again. She is there still, an active and capable woman who cares for her children well.

LYDIA NDHLOVU saw her husband go off to Johannesburg the year after they were married. He came back once, returned to Johannesburg and disappeared, leaving Lydia with two small children. She found out at last where he was, left her children with her people, sold an ox to pay for her journey, and after days of searching in Johannesburg found her husband. She refused to go home without him. At last he persuaded her to return to the children, promising to follow soon. He never came. Lydia waited five years and then lost heart. She went to the missionary who was her friend and threw her marriage certificate on his table. " That is no use to me," she said. " I must go my own way as I have no husband." A little later she entered into a pagan marriage and has been heard of no more.

SABINA was a child of the mission. She was married in church and by *lobolo* to Samuel, a Christian boy. At first he loved her very much, but he went to work in Johannesburg. The excitements of town life were too much for him ; he forgot Sabina, fell in love with a smartly dressed girl in Johannesburg and took her as his wife. He sent no money, or clothes, or letters to Sabina. The little wife often wept in her village. She and her lovely baby boy lived with relations while the long sad months went by. At last, when his contract at the mines was over, Samuel came home. His friends at the mission were able to show him how wrong he had been. Samuel repented, Sabina forgave him, they lived together again. They have now a second baby boy. It is nearly time for Samuel to go to the mines again. Will he, this time, be faithful to his wife and his home ?

In the back of a church in a certain mission station a sad-faced young African woman can be seen with a little baby in her arms. Several years ago, as a bright girl, MADDALINA was married to Philip. He went to Johannesburg for work. Years passed by. He never sent money to pay the hut tax or to provide his wife with food or clothes. He completely forgot her and took another woman as his wife. Maddalina held out for a long weary time. Then she yielded to temptation. The little baby in her arms is not Philip's child. The man who is its father did a cruel thing in tempting some one so lonely and so sad. Perhaps he and Philip will both repent some day as poor Maddalina is repenting now.

I have on my desk a word-picture sent by a white teacher in Natal from a place where she has lived for long. Thirty years ago, she tells us, the women, even the Christians, could not read or write. The husband alone had authority in the house. A boy over six years old was free from his mother's control. The wives walked humbly some yards behind their husbands, carrying all the loads. Unmarried girls dare not go for a walk without a brother to protect them. Bigger children began to come to school, but they seldom got beyond a little Zulu reading and writing and very simple arithmetic.

Now, thirty years later, an enormous change has come. The women have been in contact with white people from the West. They have been left in sole charge of house and children while most of the men have been away for nine months of the year working in towns or mines. The women have learned to stand on their own feet.

It is not uncommon for younger women to have passed the sixth or seventh standard in school. They can speak and write English. They order their houses in a civilised way and make clothes for their children. Young men send their young wives, or the girls they mean to marry, to be taught. They desire a higher standard of living and only the women can give them that.

The young man and his wife now walk side by side. He often carries his share of the load. He has even been seen to raise his hat as he greets a girl. The young educated mother holds her own with her children and is no longer despised for her ignorance by her little son.

This white woman of long experience looks not

only at the past and the present, she looks also into the future for her African friends. The pace is almost too rapid, she says ; there is danger in the breaking up of tribal and family custom and control. Hitherto marriage has been the lot of every girl. But now many say openly that they do not want to be under a husband's control. Polygamy is dying out and in a few years there will be a number of unmarried women in middle life. What will they make of their lives ? The desire for freedom of action needs to be directed into pathways of service.

IV

DR. AGGREY'S VIEW

There are people, both white and black, who are inclined to think that the great changes in Africa have brought more loss than gain. They would bring back the old days if they could. Dr. Aggrey often talked about this. He was sure that on the whole his country had gained. It was a pride to him that Africa had gold and rich ore in her soil. He felt that the treasures of the land should be opened up for the use of the world. He was glad that the white man had come to Africa, for he was convinced that black and white people could do together what neither could do alone. He spoke plainly of faults in both races, which made it difficult for them to be friends. He knew that unfair advantage was sometimes taken of his own people. When he travelled himself in Africa trying things happened, as may be read in his life.[1]

[1] *Aggrey of Africa.* By E. W. Smith. London : Student Christian Movement.

But anger found no place in his mind. His deep belief in the justice of the best white people made him sure that misunderstandings and barriers would be removed. He worked without ceasing to raise African men and women to a higher level of knowledge and experience so that black and white might go forward together.

Here was an African well fitted to strike a balance between gain and loss. He was a student of African history and of the history of the world. He had seen the relation of black and white races being worked out in the United States where Negroes were steadily winning their way and overcoming heavy disabilities with patient courage. In his veins ran the blood of many West African chiefs. He counted among his personal friends some of the best white men and women and the best black men and women too. He knew the inner side of life in many parts of Africa and wherever he touched indolence or injustice his spirit burned with indignation at the wrong, whether done by white or black. It was this great African, steeped in the past and bound up in the progress of the present, who urged his people to welcome the good that the new day in Africa had brought, especially to the women, and to set themselves with patient hope to overcome the bad results of change. To him, with his burning faith in the part which sons and daughters of Africa might play, the golden day of Africa—" my Africa "—lay not in the past but in the future.

PART II

LINKING THE OLD AND THE NEW

CHAPTER 6

PREPARATION FOR LIFE

I

THINGS AFRICA HAS DONE

IN changing Africa, so full of things old and new, a choice has constantly to be made between what is to be kept and what is to be let go. Some of the old things are so precious that Africa will be spoiled if they are lost. But young Africans have to move forward and live their lives in the new day. They cannot go back to all the ways of their fathers and their ancestors. But they can find out all that was best in the old life and customs and carry it forward into the new day.

Tribal Africa has given a large place to the preparation of boys and girls for life, first in the duties learned at home and from the elders of the tribe, and then in the initiation schools.

A tiny girl in her West African home copies the doings of her mother. She learns to balance a water-pot on her little head. She imitates her mother as she rubs the walls and floor of her house with clay water and a handful of banana fibre. She sees the way boiled yams are pounded. Soon she begins to do these things herself. Then she helps to sift and winnow dry beans in a wicker tray. A little later she gains skill in the shaping of water-pots and even begins to do something in the market place. By the time a girl is twelve years old she has learned these things, and many others. No one can measure how much this home preparation for life has meant.

Up to this time, learning the day's work has kept the child's mind active, but when she has mastered what daily life requires she has only to do the same things over and over again, year after year. Unless she goes to school, no world of thought and knowledge opens before the African child. Girlhood, with its wealth of new interests, such as comes to girls in the western world is not part of African life. As the body of a child only grows and develops through food and exercise, so the mind only grows if it has fresh food for thought and fresh things to do.

Sometimes in Africa the longing to know how to do things is like a great pain to a woman who has never had a chance to learn. A well-known white man in Uganda tells a story about this. One day a little girl, who was a servant of KING MWANGA'S MOTHER, came to him with a strange request. Her mistress wished him to write a letter to this little servant, as if it were a letter from the Queen Mother herself, and sign it with the Queen Mother's name. The missionary was very busy. But it was easier to write the letter than to argue with the little girl. So the letter

was written and taken back to the Queen Mother's court.

Long weeks afterwards the same little girl came back and told the missionary she had had a letter from her mistress. Would he read it to her ? At first he thought the child had brought his own letter back again. But no ! He looked closely, and found the second letter had been written by someone else. Then he discovered that the Queen Mother had been longing to know how to write. The only way she could learn was to get a letter written by some one and copy it over and over again. She had never learned writing but she made in the end a perfect copy of every word.

African tribes in many places have initiation schools. In some of these, things are done to the bodies of young people which are very painful and even dangerous to life. Some such customs connected with the schools are happily beginning to pass away. There are tribes which still use initiation rites for girls which cause great suffering. They may also make it very difficult for the girl when she marries to be a healthy mother.

As knowledge of the laws of health and of the various parts of the human body spreads in Africa, the people themselves are beginning to give up the hurtful customs which are mixed with many of the initiation schools. Already there is a difference of opinion among Africans on this subject. Moshoeshoe, the great chief of the Basuto, believed in the schools, but he never let a school be held unless he could be there himself. Chief Khama of Bechuanaland, one of the greatest of African rulers, was opposed to the schools. He let no child of his pass through them and made no secret of his dislike to their influence on boys and girls.

Dr. Aggrey, who loved everything that was African, saw the tremendous power of these schools. He wanted to stop their relation with medicine men and magic. He spoke often of things he wanted to see changed. He felt that in some initiation schools boys were taught to look on women as inferior to themselves, useful only to bear children and do the work of the family, and girls were sometimes taught to look on themselves only as the property of the men. He desired something better than that for Africa. But he felt that to hold properly worked schools to introduce boys and girls to the meaning of life was good and right. The plan was one of the wise things which Africa had given to the world.

Now that African leaders are thinking about this subject there is hope that the needed change will come. For the present, in tribes where the old rites prevail, African Christians do not let their children enter the tribal school.

The truth behind these schools and many other practices now falling out of use in Africa is well worth carrying forward to the new day. It is a good and worthy thing that boys and girls should be taught the duties and responsibilities of manhood and womanhood as they stand on the border of life. It is good that at a suitable time girls should be solemnly prepared for the sacred duties of marriage and parenthood. In some ways ancient Africa has paid more heed to this than many lands in the West.

II

SOME NEW ENDEAVOURS

Sons and daughters of Africa, in partnership with their white friends, are building a bridge from the past to the new present in many helpful ways. Here is the story of one.

In the diocese of MASASI in Tanganyika a new

CHE SARA, A LEADER IN THE MALANGO

kind of initiation school, under the direction of the bishop and the African elders of the Church, has been held for several years. These schools are welcomed both by the tribe and by the Christian Church. The rites are like the old ones, but they are free from all that is hurtful to mind or body.

White missionaries at present take part in the schools, but one day they will be entirely in African hands. Even now Christian chiefs take a leading part. Teaching is given by African men to the boys, by African women to the girls. The picture of Che Sara, feeding a motherless baby, shows what these teachers are like. She is trusted and valued ; the white missionaries say she has taught them much.

The boys' rite lasts for several weeks. The girls' camp only goes on for ten days. After a special service in church, where all the people pray for them, the girls who are going into the *malango* (so their school is called) walk in procession to their camp. They sleep and eat in the enclosure which is made for them. Teaching is given them twice a day. In the year 1930 some 400 girls came to be initiated. Most of the other girls and women between fifteen and twenty years of age have now passed through the school. The teachers whom the girls have with them are Christian African matrons like Che Sara, carefully chosen and not very old. With them are generally younger matrons in training for this special work. The girls are taught the conduct becoming to a maiden and how evil may be avoided. Each girl, with her mother's approval, has explained to her privately the change which comes in her body when she passes out of childhood into womanhood.

Boys and girls, each in their own school, are given the same teaching about their moral life. They are taught what truth means. They learn how noble it is to be always worthy to be trusted and not to fail anyone who puts confidence in them. They learn about purity, and the need for bodily self-control. They learn about the sin of bad conversation and the duty of resisting evil thoughts. They are taught about Christian betrothal and marriage, so that they may turn away from any unworthy customs of youth which may still prevail in the tribe. The danger of indulging in strong drink is made plain.

Wise Africans come in to teach the ways of showing respect to elders which are observed in the tribe. The honour of work for the cultivation of the soil is taught. The joy and duty of worshipping God are in the centre of the teaching in the schools.

On the eleventh day, newly bathed and in new clothes, the girl initiates walk in procession to the church to a special service in which a blessing is given to them. When they leave the church and meet their friends and relatives there is great rejoicing. Such of the tribal dances as Christians can rightly join in then take place.

Following the custom of the tribe, the Church at Masasi has arranged four rites as the girl's life goes on to marriage and into motherhood. The first rite is held in the camp. All the others are held by the African woman teacher in the girl's own home. Her mother is present, or her husband after she has married. Each rite leads up to a special service in church.

When the girl becomes adult an official record is made of the fact. She is taught more fully the respect due to the body which God has given her. She is taught the meaning of betrothal and the right bearing of a girl towards men. This teaching is given in her home. Then, with her mother, her relatives and her friends she is brought to church and kneels in front of the people. The African woman teacher says :

" We pray the blessing of God for this our child now come to years of discretion."

Then prayers are offered. From them we take these beautiful words :

" Almighty God, we give Thee hearty thanks that Thou hast mercifully guarded this maiden through the years of her childhood and hast brought her safely to this day. We beseech Thee in Thy mercy to grant that she may continue to abide in Thy keeping and enjoy the fulness of Thy blessing in soul and body. Guard her in every temptation of evil and save her from all the wiles of the devil. . . . If Thou call her to the married life we beseech Thee to fill her household with the joy of Thy blessing. . . . Through Jesus Christ our Lord. Amen."

The *malango* at Masasi is one of the new endeavours to prepare African girls for life. But there are many more.

Ever since white women began to go as missionary teachers to Africa their homes have been places where the African girl could carry on the training her mother began. Many girls who begin by helping a white mother in the care of her children and of her house get a real preparation for a home of their own. The love between the white women and the girls they have trained in their houses often lasts through life.

There are many schools in Africa which aim at preparing children and girls for life. I will tell you about one of these. The school is at MBERESHI in Northern Rhodesia. The girls are brought by their parents when they are five or six years old. Many of them stay till they are married at eighteen or nineteen years of age. They live in a number

of small houses in the compound round the school.
An elder girl is the " mother " of each little household, the next eldest is the " aunt." The children,
about a dozen in each house, are of all ages just
as they would be in a family. The mother divides
the duties of her household among all the members.

GIRLS TRAINED AT MBERESHI SCHOOL

Even the youngest, who may perhaps be only five
years old, has something special to do. The
duties are changed every month so that each child
learns all that has to be done. Once a day the
mother leads her family with pots or buckets on
their heads to draw water for the house. Twice
a week she takes her axe and the family follow her
to the forest to get firewood. Every afternoon she

takes the children to the bathing place, where they are well soaped and plunged into the fresh cool water. Every Sunday morning she anoints them with oil till their skins look soft and beautiful like dark velvet. She prepares food for any child who is ill and cares for her. She and the aunt wash all the garments for their household and mend clothes and blankets. Each member of the family makes the one simple cotton garment she wears.

Each mother tries to make her house foremost in order, cleanliness, and beauty. All the mothers and aunts are responsible for the school village. They help in the sanitary arrangements of the school. In the school gardens there is abundance of everything the African woman has in hers. Except the hard digging all the work in the gardens is done by the girls.

The mothers and aunts meet as " elders of the village " and are always in close and constant touch with the white missionary women who work with them and through them. Each one feels responsible for the whole community. The children learn to worship the " Great Chief " Jesus Christ and bring his spirit into the school. Do you wonder that there are many young men who want to marry the girls who have had this sort of preparation for life ? Surely they and their husbands will be worthy builders in Africa's new day.

III

THE STORY OF FANNY I. AMÉ

In some parts of Africa, where the education of boys is ahead of that provided for girls, another

kind of school is found. All the pupils are elder
girls already engaged to be married. These
training schools for girls before marriage really
mean that public opinion in Africa is changing.
The number of men who wish for educated wives
is increasing year by year. Of course, wives who
could cook, till the garden, and bear children have
always been wanted. But this is something more.
The standard for home life is rising. A man wants
a wife who can be his companion and share his
interests. He wants his children to have a good
start in life. If he is a Christian, he wants a
Christian wife. In the old days fathers, brothers,
and husbands were not willing that girls should go
to school. That mistaken idea lives on here and
there. But it is dying out. One of the proofs of
that fact is the number of training homes for
future wives which are springing up, mainly in
West Africa.

Perhaps the best known of these is in the district
of the Long Ju-Ju in Calabar, Southern Nigeria,
the home of Mbafo and Mboro, whose stories you
read in Chapter 3. It is called after Mary Slessor,
the wonderful little missionary from Scotland, who
by love made friends with warrior chiefs and
tamed savage tribes. Most of the pupils are girls
engaged to be married. They are given simple
teaching. They do all the work of the school
compound and cultivate food and fruit on the farm.
They gain experience in the care of little children
and babies, a trained nurse teaches them about
health. The Slessor Home is a happy, busy place.
Everyone gives willing service. Work is a privi-
lege which the healthy girls enjoy. A visitor once
saw a girl weeping bitterly on the matron's

veranda. She learned that the girl had been very naughty and had been left to spend the day alone in idleness instead of doing a morning's work with her schoolmates on the farm. This is the only punishment ever used in the home !

In a district in the Ibo country, also in Southern Nigeria, a white missionary woman began a home to train girls for marriage and home life some years ago, because there were many educated Christian lads and few girls for them to marry. After a time she had to leave West Africa and spend three years in England. What was to be done ? Scores of girls were waiting for training and there was no white woman to do the work. So the Church turned to the African women who had helped the missionary. One was put in charge of girls at the central home. Others were scattered through the district in charge of houses where they took in girls and women and taught them what they could. The Church members built these houses, maintained them, and paid the teachers' salaries. The food for the girls was paid for by the future husbands. The teachers were not wise or learned but they had the gift of leadership. They did faithfully for the girls what the central home had done for themselves. At last the white missionary came back and found the houses filled with girls. The number of houses still grows as more African women are ready to be put in charge.

Here is the story of one African woman, whose work stands out above the rest. Her name is Mrs. FANNY I. AMÉ. Her life sometimes reminds us of that of Samuel Adjai Crowther, the first African bishop of the Niger.[1]

---

[1] See *Lives of Eminent Africans*, pp. 65–77.

Between thirty and forty years ago a slave trader came down the River Niger to Asaba, bringing with him two children, a boy and a girl. They looked so unhappy that a kind-hearted white official in the Niger Company's police redeemed them. He gave them to a missionary, who put the little girl with the wife of a good pastor from Sierra Leone. She was a true mother to the child. A few years later the girl went on to the house of a white missionary. Then she married an African engineer on a boat on the river. In 1911 her husband died, leaving her three small houses. The rent of these was enough for her support.

Then Mrs. Amé entered on what proved to be a splendid life-work. She began first as helper in a newly opened home for girls. As the work grew, her powers grew with it until she became unpaid matron in charge of the whole work. The house, in a large compound between the two main roads to the market in Onitsha, was soon used entirely to train girls for married life. The matron knows not only her ninety girls but the young men they are to marry—artisans, houseboys, motor-drivers, sometimes a clerk from a store.

Under Mrs. Amé's care the girls learn the duties of a simple home. They learn to read the Ibo language ; if there is time they learn some English and how to write. They are prepared to join the Christian Church to which their future husbands belong. The girls live in African fashion, cooking and marketing for themselves. Like their matron they wear gay cotton dresses with a silk handkerchief or a bright cotton scarf wound round their heads. It is a fine sight to see the vigorous, brightly clad girls gathered with the matron for their Wednesday afternoon Bible Class.

The little girl brought in bondage down the river has become a woman respected in all the districts round. White residents in Onitsha are her friends. Hundreds of African girls who have passed through her home look on her as their second mother. Hundreds of African youths bless her for the training given to prepare their chosen girls for married life. Scores of neat, well-kept little African homes where happy children play are being set up by young couples who have taken Mrs. Amé as their guide.

This steady, useful life was suddenly flooded with romance. Mrs. Amé heard of the long-lost relatives whom she had never traced. It was a wonderful joy. She went to the place in the Udi district where her people were. There was great rejoicing and killing of goats. Her fame had gone through the country, so her people were proud to welcome her. She brought some of her relatives, who had remained entirely in the bush and followed the old ways, to see her friends in Onitsha. She took three of her brother's children to live with her and will bring them up herself. She is giving money towards the support of a teacher among her people.

We leave Mrs. Amé with her home full of girls, happy in her new-found relations. A pleasing picture is given of this daughter of Africa : she is of medium height, her round pleasant face often lit by a winning smile ; a woman strong, determined, able to control. Quick in judgment and forceful in speech, her true sympathy and quiet bearing win the confidence of old and young.

CHAPTER 7

MARRIED LIFE AND MOTHERHOOD

I

THREE AFRICAN LOVE STORIES

HERE are three African love stories which girls shortly to be married will like to read in preparation for coming days. One is the story of an old Bushman and his wife, another is a lovely tale of long ago in Zululand, the third is the picture of a young husband and wife in their West African home.

Karinna and Kouke

Many young Africans have scarcely heard of the Bushmen, those strange, wild, little people who lived in parts of the southern half of the continent. They shot their poisoned arrows at Hottentot and Bantu and were cruelly treated in return. These Bushmen were low down in the human scale, but they had something hidden away in them that was great and beautiful. They left wonderful pictures in many places, on rocks and in caves. The animals they drew looked as if they were alive. Very few Bushmen are left ; they have almost died out.

A well-known South African writer was interested in the Bushmen and wanted to understand their pictures. He had copies made of some of them and inquired where any of the remaining Bushmen could be found. He heard that an old man named KARINNA, and KOUKE his wife, were living in a cave in Basutoland, just across the border of the Orange Free State, under the protection of a kindly neighbour. He went to see them and came upon what I call a love story. I wonder what you will think! Some of the love stories I like best belong to the end of life as well as to the beginning.

Karinna and Kouke were old and poor, having lost kinsfolk, children, and home. But the visitor could see that they were still a pair of lovers, happy together in their old age. He showed them copies of the cave paintings by some of their own people. Their eyes shone with joy. The old woman began to sing some of the half-forgotten Bushman songs. Her husband begged her to stop, it hurt him to have his memory stirred. He touched her arm and said, " Don't, don't! It makes my heart too sad." But she sang on, and at last he joined in the singing. Then she began the song of a dance for hunters. The old man went behind the visitor's waggon, decked his old head with arrows, and, nodding in time to the music, danced as his wife sang.

They were only remnants of a despised and persecuted race. But some of the greatest things in life were theirs. Many kings and queens might envy them.

This story of the old Bushman couple who loved each other is told in a big book which can be seen in great libraries in Cape Town, in London, and elsewhere.

Nomlingo and Bahu

The next love story is from Zululand. NOM-LINGO, the daughter of Mala, was a beautiful girl. Two young men wished to marry her. One of them, named Bahu, was a hunter of elephants and giraffes, but he had no cattle with which to pay the father of the girl. The other, Mafisi, was rich, and offered a hundred head of cattle in exchange for his bride. Mala gladly accepted his offer, but Nomlingo wept, for Bahu, poor though he was, had won her heart.

The girl's tears moved her father to change his mind. " Choose then, for yourself, my child," he said. " But mark ! He whom you choose must beat all others in wrestling, throwing the spear, and running, or he cannot have my daughter as his wife."

The people all gathered outside the kraal to watch the contest for Nomlingo. At the last moment Mala handed his daughter a necklace of charms sewn in tiny bags of crocodile skin. " Take this, my child," he said, " and put it round the neck of the man you choose." Nomlingo passed by Mafisi and put the charm round Bahu's neck. This act of hers gave him double strength ; he determined that he would win.

The wrestling began. With wonderful power Bahu threw one man after another to the ground. Then the large, soft, round root of a certain plant was rolled down the slope and each man tried to stab it with his assegai. Suddenly a duiker buck broke out of the covert and dashed across the line. Mafisi hastily threw his assegai and grazed it on the leg. Bahu, pausing to take aim, sent his blade straight into the duiker's lungs.

Then old Mala set the final test. He pointed to a round hill of sand on the south side of St. Lucia Bay rising high and bare above the flat land, with bushes round its lower part. For thirty miles around it can be seen; it is still known as Kwa Bahu. " Who first gets to the top of that hill," said Mala, " shall have my daughter as his bride."

THE FINAL TEST—BAHU LEADS

There, on the crown of the hill, stood Nomlingo, waiting with her mother by her side.

One youth after another started eagerly, passing round the bushes, leaping the ditches, plunging down into the gullies and up again. But only two got to the last steep slope of the sandy hill—Mafisi, with white cow-tails hanging from his elbows, Bahu, with white ostrich plumes on his head streaming in the breeze. Side by side they panted on. The men looked upward from below; the two women downward from above. Little by little Mafisi fell into the background ; step by step Bahu gained ground. At last with one great effort he reached Nomlingo, grasped her by the hand, and fell speechless at her feet. Blood flowed from his nose and mouth. She bathed his chest and face with water, but he died in her arms. Then, as the men below gazed up anxiously at the hill-top, a soft mist rose gently round it and hid the scene from view.

The girl wrapped her lover's corpse in her mantle and, half-wild with grief, tried to dig with her hands a grave for him in the sand. No one but herself might touch his body or tread on the ground where he lay. Tenderly and alone she made his grave and laid him in it, covering him from sight. Then she laid herself upon the mound and mourned far into the night, till at last she was still.

Her mother, hidden from sight in a bush near by, crept out noiselessly in the darkness and laid a skin kaross over the girl. When morning dawned she called softly, " Nomlingo ? " But the girl lay cold and lifeless. She had followed the one she loved into the spirit land. Soon the father and mother laid her body by her lover, and left them there in peace.

Every day since then, when a soft mist creeps at noon over Kwa Bahu, the old Zulu story of Bahu and Nomlingo is brought to mind.

Margaret in her Home

The third love story can be read between the lines of this letter which has come from a friend— herself rather like Margaret—in West Africa.

" It is early morning and MARGARET did not
know we were coming, but her house is always in
order. Never have I seen a house so expressive of
gaiety and good-humour. She has stained the
floors and a twelve-inch border round the walls
quite black. Above that the walls are of snowy
whiteness, finished at the top with another border
of black. Red and white curtains flap in the
breeze at Margaret's windows and she has taken
the same material to make cushions for her chairs.

" Next door is the school where Margaret's
husband, as headman, rules over three hundred
boys, nine girls, and half a dozen young assistant
teachers. They are short of teachers and Margaret
is trying to make up her mind to take one of the
infant classes. We talk about this bold project.
She taught infants before her marriage and would
like to do so again, but no woman in the Ibo
country has ever taught school after marriage.
But this slim girl with shining eyes has the spirit
of a pioneer.

" Her husband comes to greet us and sits on the
veranda wall while we talk. He is actually encouraging her to do this unheard-of thing. Only
she must be free to give up work when the next
baby comes. The present baby is nine months
old and very lovely. We cannot wonder that his
parents feel another baby after the same pattern is
essential.

" It is time for us to go and they are grieved
they have no refreshment to offer us. ' But I have
corn in my garden,' says Margaret. ' Won't you
take some of the new ears for your dinner to-
night ? ' In front of the house are neat little farm
patches of maize and yam and beans, with borders

of pine-apples and bright-leaved plants. Part belongs to the teachers, part is the school garden where the children work. Margaret goes to her own plot and raises her slim round arms to pluck the highest corn from a tall stalk.

" Her cotton dress is a mixture of orange and brown and gold. The cloth round her head is rose and dull blue. The sun pours down upon her. As she stands there in the brightness, her small head thrown back, her smiling face upraised, her dark eyes opening fearlessly upon the full glory of the morning, she seems to me the perfect picture of our hopes for Africa.

" Here, in the heart of a bush town—a town so well known for its revolting practices that its neighbours shun it—a man and a girl are building a home. Youth and honest joy and simple faith and serviceable knowledge are at work. The home is so simple that the wildest man from the bush comes without hesitation to sit sociably on its doorstep. It is a home so gay and cleanly that the dullest girl from the bush must look upon it with wonder and with hope."

II

SOME MOTHERS : THE SEKIBOBO'S WIFE AT HOME

We are now going to visit a happy home in Uganda. Those who have read the life of Sir Apolo Kagwa,[1] the Prime Minister of Uganda, will remember his great visit to England to see King Edward VII crowned. With him came one

[1] See *Lives of Eminent Africans*, pp. 90–105.

MRS. SALA MUKASA'S HAPPY HOME IN UGANDA

of the chiefs of Uganda, who afterwards wrote a book about the visit. His name is Ham Mukasa ; he is the Sekibobo or head chief of Kyagwe, a large province of Uganda. His wife is SALA MUKASA, daughter of one of the best chiefs Uganda has ever had. She was among the first girls educated in the Gayaza High School. She passed from one happy home to another, and is helping her husband in all his work. Seven fine high-spirited boys and girls make Nasuti, as the Seki-bobo's house is called, a lively place.

The first thing visitors notice about the Mukasa household is the way the children play. The centre of the house is a large round room or hall where guests are received. The children love the big arm-chairs and climb up into them, pushing one another out in fun. Then they dash off to the smooth grass lawns where their father has built a nursery play-house for them. Out come their favourite tricycles on which the children ride round and round with merry laughter. On Sunday mornings they are much more sedate. They go off to Sunday school in the motor car, each child bearing a little bag with money for the collection. At the door the driver lifts the children down, the little nursemaids follow, and James Hannington, the eldest son, called after the martyred bishop, leads a well-behaved procession into school. The parents keep a big book into which the mother puts the wise and merry sayings of the children.

In some ways Nasuti is a very modern house ; in others it is thoroughly African. Busy as the mistress is with her children, her guests, her husband's work and her own, she goes out at sunrise every morning to dig and plant the household's food supply, helps in cooking the native meals, and by her example shows other wives the dignity of labour.

This happy wife and mother wants other wives and mothers to be happy too. So she works a branch of a great union of mothers, which is active not only in Uganda but in all the world. Weekly meetings are held in her house. Twenty or thirty women may be seen seated upon the matted floor while Sala Mukasa, or some other member, speaks to them. One day the Sekibobo came home, and as he drew near the open window of his room he heard a voice speaking. It was one of the African members of the Mothers' Union addressing the rest. She was talking about marriage. The great chief listened amazed and delighted. " People do not know about this wisdom which is in married women," he afterwards said. When the speech was over the women prayed. Ham Mukasa knelt by his open window and prayed with them too.

Being a true mother, Sala Mukasa cares for the children of other mothers as well as for her own. At Christmas time her Mothers' Union gives a great children's party with a splendid Christmas tree laden with gifts. She visits the girls' school regularly and helps the African schoolmistress with wise advice. One year she went with her husband to the prize-giving at the central boys' school. She distributed the prizes and gave the boys an address on the need for guarding their thoughts during the holidays. No woman had ever done such a thing before in Uganda.

Here are stories of two other good African mothers.

The African who listened to the speakers in

Hyde Park, London (see p. 49), has sent the story of his mother for this book. She was the daughter of one of the first converts in the American mission in Zululand. She was trained in the house of one of the pioneer missionaries. In course of time she married James Dube, the pastor of the Inanda Church. Her name was Elizabeth Nomanzi Dube. After nine children had been born the husband and father died. It was a large family to be dependent on a mother, but by hard work she managed to educate every one. She sent three sons to America for further study. Two of them became well-known leaders among their own people. One of them, her son John, who has written to us, is founder and principal of the Ohlange Institute, near Inanda. The Christian character of this devoted mother was a power in her own home and her influence reached many others. When she died one of the friends who spoke at her funeral said, " She has done more than any other person in our community to educate children."

Quite another type of African mother is Dorcas, the wife of Lisasi, who still lives at Yalemba on the Congo. Her early life was exciting. She was taken captive in a fight between her own village and another. Her mother ran to rescue her but was killed on the path. The chief who conquered her village took the child to sell her to the soldiers, but a state official stopped him and gave her into the care of a missionary. Dorcas was at first a naughty little girl but afterwards became a true Christian. Out of the many men who wanted to marry her she chose Lisasi, and she chose well. He was first the captain of the little steamer *Grenfell*, then he settled in a village with Dorcas. They had four fine healthy children, so Lisasi was able to live tax free. The Belgian Government offered freedom from taxation to any man who had one wife and four or more healthy children. Only one other couple in the village could claim this.

Dorcas is like a mother to the whole village. She cares for the mothers when their babies are born. She makes peace in family quarrels. The grown-up girls flock to her and she advises them all. She walks among the people of the village with quiet dignity and grace. The whole district knows what a wife she is to Lisasi and how much her help and comradeship mean. It is said among the neighbours, "Dorcas and Lisasi have no quarrels at all." But it is among her children that Dorcas is seen at her best. She enters into all their play. She can "make believe" as well as they can. She never "talks down" to them. She and they understand one another. Yet she is not only a playmate but a strong wise mother who trains them in worthy ways.

III

The Story of Rola Oluwole : By her Mother

Mrs. Oluwole, wife of the African Assistant Bishop of the Lagos Diocese in West Africa, has brought up five daughters and one son to serve their own people. All her children had part of their education in England, following teaching given at home by their mother and then in African schools. In this happy family the friendship was so strong between two of the daughters, ROLA and Ronke, that they were like twins. Together they went to school in England, and now that Rola's bright and joyful life has ended, Ronke tries to take her place. In order that other girls in Africa may see what Rola's life was like, her mother has written her story for this book. It is given in her own words.

" Rola was born on March 4th, 1896. Her first name, Martha, was after her paternal grandmother. Her second name, Kofoworola, means ' she does not buy honour but is born in it.' This was given because she was the first child born after my husband became a bishop. An English woman missionary friend of mine, who was fond of the baby, could not pronounce her name correctly so called her ' Rola.' To please baby's friend, we all did the same.

" From her infancy to her death, Rola was always bright, lively, sweet-tempered, and sun-shiny. When she was six years old, I began to teach her the alphabet. She got on so rapidly that in six months I was advised to stop her lessons. I did so and then taught her to occupy her time in sweeping, dusting, sewing, doing fancy needle-work. She also played indoor games, and enjoyed skipping and running out of doors. When she was eight we sent her as a day scholar to a good school. Before she was fourteen she was the head girl. She soon began teaching in the same school and received her first salary in December, 1910. She carried on her studies after school hours and attended teachers' lectures given by government educationists. In due course she obtained the government first-class teachers' certificate and finally became the senior African teacher of her old school. In addition to teaching subjects like Scripture, reading, geography, and arithmetic, she taught native cookery in all its branches.

" Rola and her youngest sister Ronke, now Mrs. Lucas, left for England in May, 1920, and returned home three years later. They spent a year at an English school, taking lessons in literature, type-writing, singing, and pianoforte. The second year they spent in a theological college. The third year was spent in London taking advanced lessons in English cookery, laundry, and scientific dress-making. The two girls enjoyed their visit to England immensely, as well as two fortnights spent in Paris and in Belgium.

" On their return home they at once threw themselves into work. They found many parents distressed through not having a school to which to send their children. The demand for education was so great that all the schools were full, with a long waiting list of pupils. Children sometimes had to wait a year or more before they could be admitted. Rola and Ronke opened a school which was called ' The Misses Oluwole's Private School and Domestic Economy Class.' Pupils from five to sixteen years of age were taught Scripture and the usual school subjects. Two of them in due course passed the preliminary examination of the College of Preceptors in England. In the domestic economy class for pupils from about sixteen to twenty, English and African cookery in all branches, scientific dressmaking, plain and fancy needlework, and, in the case of boarders laundry work, were taught.

" At the first prize day, December, 1923, the

school had about 50 pupils ; the following year it had nearly 100. Ronke left then to prepare for her wedding, but the prize days of December, 1925, and the following year, found Rola with about 130 pupils in her school. On the recommendation of the Government Director of Education, Rola was appointed a member of the Board of Education in Nigeria, the only African woman yet so honoured. The Governor's wife presided at the last prize day of the school, which was then closed to enable Rola to prepare for her marriage.

" Rola, like her sisters, taught regularly in the Sunday school. The vicar of the church asked her to help him to carry on the young women's Bible class of the parish. Rola threw her heart so eagerly into this work that the class grew considerably and the members loved her. She also formed a musical club for educated girls. About a dozen elder married women were patrons and the club met once a month in turn at their houses. At the meetings club members sang or played the piano, and at the end of each year the club gave an evening social with music, recitations, games, and delicious refreshments.

" When Rola was married in December, 1926, she had a very nice wedding. The couple spent a few weeks at a pretty farm some miles away from Lagos for their honeymoon. Rola and her husband, the Rev. C. A. Sowunmi, settled down in their new home quite happily ; but, alas ! Rola gave birth to a still-born child in September, 1927, and died a few days later, aged thirty-one."

CHAPTER 8

TWO TALES

HERE are two stories of daughters of Africa which begin in childhood and carry on right through life. Both women belong to well-known tribes, Zulu in the south, Fanti in the west. One was the daughter of a chief and began life in a country kraal ; the other is daughter of a leading African merchant on the Gold Coast and was partly educated in England. The story of Noma-mbotwe was written down by an American missionary. Christine Simango, at the request of her friend who writes this book, has told for us the story of her own life.

I

IN ZULU KRAALS

The Story of Noma-mbotwe

Two little Zulu sisters quarrelled loudly as they stood upon the platform of their grass watch tower. Meantime the birds and monkeys were busy in the cornfields which the sisters were supposed to protect by throwing stones at the intruders. As one child tried to push the other off the platform, their mother, armed with a stick, came up through the tall stalks of waving corn. Seizing Noma-mbotwe by the arm she struck her again and again on her bare back and shoulders. No wonder she was angry, for the monkeys had eaten most of the corn she had hoed and weeded with her own hands. Noma tried to explain that she had really been busy throwing stones, but that her younger sister would not help her. But Noma was not her mother's favourite and blows fell sharply again.

A sudden twist, and Noma broke free from her mother and fled home for refuge to her father the chief. Panting and sobbing she appealed to him for aid. " I have had enough of this sort of thing," he said. " If your mother whips you again I will send you to the mission station at Umzumbe to live with my friends there."

A few days later, Noma, just ten years old, was brought to the missionary's door by a tall young Zulu. He gave the little girl to her father's friend and went back to the kraal. Noma had a bath in the river; her tangled hair was cut off and she was given a bright, simple cotton frock. When she saw herself in the glass she stood spell-bound. But oh! how frightened she was! She crept about the house like a little deer from the bush. The missionary with " windows on her eyes " was so alarming that Noma wanted to run away.

The Zulu child quickly grew into a bright girl, full of energy, always ready for fun. In her heart a little flame of love began to burn for the Saviour Jesus, of whom the friend of her father spoke. There were many other Zulu girls at Umzumbe who lived in a big house with several teachers.

One day a great heathen chief who had many wives and herds of cattle arrived in splendid Zulu dress. He wanted another wife and asked for Noma-mbotwe. She shook her head and sent him away. Other offers of marriage came. Noma refused them all. At last she lost her heart to a fine young Zulu named Muhle, who was working for the missionary. He was good to look at and very lively, just what Noma liked. His father was rich and could give many cattle for her. But the beginning of love to God in her heart made her troubled, for Muhle was a heathen still. She said, " I cannot marry you, for I am a Christian." But Muhle had a plan. He persuaded Noma that if she went back to her father's house and pretended to be a heathen his father would provide the fifteen cows Noma's father wanted, and the wedding could be arranged in Zulu fashion. As soon as the marriage was over and the cows were paid, Muhle promised he would become a Christian and bring Noma back to live at Umzumbe.

All that was wild and daring in Noma caught at such an adventure as this. The little voice in her heart seemed to get weaker till it could scarcely be heard. She slipped away from her home in Umzumbe. The women in her father's house eagerly adorned her again as a Zulu girl.

Presently Muhle asked to have her as his bride. Her father, old Chief Nkumbi, though he was a heathen still with many wives, was full of sorrow because his " little princess," as he called her, had turned back to the old Zulu way. But Noma checked her fears and flung herself into all the customs of an ancient Zulu wedding. The little bride danced gaily and shouted the marriage songs though she had a pain hidden away in her heart.

After the wedding Noma went to her husband's home. Being the youngest, she had to work hard for the other women in the kraal. Muhle hunted and milked the cows and attended beer drinks. Not a word was said of Umzumbe. The little inner voice in Noma's heart grew more clear. Night by night she lay awake and thought. At last she reminded her husband of his promise. Three

A ZULU MOTHER AND CHILD—UMZUMBE

times she spoke to him in vain. At last he said, " Yes, we will go back to Umzumbe."

Secretly they rolled up pots of clay and iron, wooden spoons, and blankets, inside mats. When the moon shone brightly they slipped away one night and the next morning found them at Umzumbe. They were given a place for a house. As years passed on children were born to them.

The little flame of love to God in Noma's heart burned so brightly that every one saw it.

But sorrows gathered round her. Five of her seven children died. Muhle went to work in Johannesburg and was drawn into the wickedness of the city. He never returned. Noma, alone and poor, took her baby and went to be a teacher in the Umzumbe home for girls. After four years there the call to her great life-work came.

Dweshula, headman of a district on a mountain twenty miles from Umzumbe, wanted a school. His people had been visited for years by members of the Umzumbe Church ; it was time the children should be taught. So he asked for a teacher. Noma was chosen for the work. She was not a trained teacher, but in spite of all her trouble she had still the spirit of a pioneer.

She arrived at Dweshula's, chose a grass hut for her school-house, cut two small holes in the grass walls to let in light, and invited the children to come and be taught. The mothers sent back word, " We cannot spare our children to learn the book. They are minding our babies for us." " Let them bring the babies with them," Noma replied. And they did. Seven babies arrived tied with goat skins to the bare backs of seven little sisters. Small brothers came also dressed in tiny skin aprons like their fathers and carrying little sticks and clubs.

Upon the earth floor of the grass hut Dweshula's school began. The children were bright and eager, quick to learn. All went well, except for the babies. One of them was always yelling ; sometimes several yelled at once. To carry on school was impossible. To forbid the babies to come meant losing half the scholars. Noma resolved to train the babies. She armed herself with a tiny switch. The little sisters looked on resentfully. But "Tisha" (Teacher), as they called her, was resolute. The babies thought twice before they howled. Noma became known as "the tiger of the babies." But the mothers came and thanked her for having "hushed up the country."

When the grass hut became too full the teacher and children resolved to build a school-house themselves. So each day, when the two hours' period for industrial work began, Noma and her little party went forth.

One day they plunged into deep grass and cut huge bundles of thatch for the roof. Another day they took axes, and in the dark forest two miles away they cut down poles. As tick fever had carried off all the cattle, how could the wood be pulled up the steep hills? "Tisha" harnessed the children to the poles with ropes; while they pulled, she pushed.

Posts were driven into the ground. Four strong walls of basket work were made by the children. The ridge pole was nailed on tall central poles. Dweshula's men looked on highly amused. What woman was ever known to build a house? And they laughed, Ha! Ha! No one lifted a finger to help until the house was nearly done. Then one of the men saw Noma on the top of the roof, while the children handed up the grass to her, which she sewed on with a big wooden needle. He climbed on the roof, sent away the plucky little teacher, and finished it off himself.

The framework and the roof were complete.

Noma armed the children with spades and hoes. Clay was dug and mixed into mud by the children's stout little legs so that plastering might begin. This finished, the girls pounded and polished with stones until there was a hard, smooth earth floor.

Only the white-washing remained to be done. Two miles away there was a pit where clay could be found. One afternoon Noma marched there at the head of her school. A few hours later the little troop returned carrying on their heads baskets and pots of pinkish-white clay. Very soon the ugly mud walls of the school-house were coloured like a white man's skin.

Dweshula's school-house was built. Now came the great opening day. Hundreds of guests came over the hills and through the valleys—tribesmen and tribeswomen in their best ornaments, hair freshly dressed with red clay. Except for a few people from the mission stations the whole assembly consisted of people like those who had feasted with Noma at her wild wedding. But what a contrast between the girl of that day and the woman teacher of Dweshula's school. Standing before the multitude, Noma told them of the love of God. The men looked on in amazement. They touched one another and whispered, " We have been laughing at her ! We said she could not build a house." Then they gave her a new Zulu name which meant " A giant like unto a man."

Noma became pastor as well as teacher to Dweshula's folk. Week by week the school-house service was packed with people in blankets and skins. When any were sick, " Tisha " was sent for. It was " Tisha " who told of heaven when someone died. At last one Sunday the splendid old headman himself, Dweshula, stood up in church and said, " I choose the Lord." The people loved him ; they began to want to love his God. A great awakening began. It led to new and better ways. When Dweshula died two years later Noma was with him.

" Tisha's " school advanced and prospered, until the children needed a trained teacher with a government certificate. Then she gladly handed over her school. A fine African pastor came to Dweshula's and Noma-mbotwe went to live with her grandchildren in Umzumbe. A happy old woman she was. Sunday by Sunday she loved to ride to church in a wheel-barrow. It is only a few years since she died.

II

From Gold Coast to Mozambique

The Story of Christine Simango, told by Herself

" I am a girl from the Gold Coast. My maiden name was CHRISTINE COUSSY. Our family has been well known in West Africa for several generations. My mother is descended from the same chief and stool as Dr. Aggrey. Her home was at Anamabu and on her side we consider ourselves to belong to the Fanti tribe, which has contributed a good deal to the progress of the Gold Coast.

" First, I want to say how much I owe, as well as my brothers and sisters, to the unselfishness of our parents, especially our mother. She sank her own wishes and desires and sent us thousands of miles across the sea that we might have the best

KAMBA AND CHRISTINE SIMANGO

education and culture. Now that I am a mother myself I know what heartache it must have given her.

" My earliest memories of Africa are of days at the beautiful little sea-coast town of Axim on the Gold Coast. Here for some years we lived with our parents enjoying the pleasures of sea and beach. With my brothers I went fishing and boating, joining in all their doings. Our waking hours were spent out of doors with our numerous pets. When I was six, the family moved to Cape Coast. There, as my parents were travelling on business, my sister and I went for a short time to a girls' boarding-school.

" About a year later, an aunt, who was a woman of culture and education, returned to Cape Coast after a visit to England. My sister Annie and I went to live with this aunt, attending school daily. We stayed with her in Cape Coast for two years and then she brought us with her to England.

" This, our first long sea voyage, was a great event to my sister and to me. But it was nothing to the wonders we saw and heard when we landed at Plymouth and went on to London. What a thrill our first train journey gave us ! We had never seen any kind of lights but paraffin lamps and candles. Every street and shop and lit-up house looked to us like fairyland. Every day brought some new experience to us. Our aunt took a house near London. We attended day school regularly and both learned very quickly. We enjoyed visits to the pupils at their own homes and they were welcome guests in the house of our aunt. When she returned to Africa my sister and I went to a large boarding-school in the south of

England, where we stayed for seven years. We kept pace with the other pupils in the various classes and studies and went in for the usual examinations.

" On leaving school, I gained a certificate in domestic science at a women's college. Then I took secretarial and business training in a London college, and afterwards went to work in a large business house in London with which my father was connected. Two years later I left and learned dressmaking in a London workroom. I did these things largely to gain experience of life ; they were of great service in helping me to understand people.

" When, after this long absence, I went home to the Gold Coast it was like going to a strange country. Before leaving England we arranged to help the business firm for which we had worked in a new venture in Accra. They opened a large general store like the well-known ones in London. We were to pay special attention to the departments for women and girls. Many advanced Africans came to the store as well as the simpler people. We had a splendid opportunity of getting to know our own people during the three years we worked in that store.

" It would take too long to tell the many humorous incidents which took place. On certain days the people came to town from the small interior villages. At that time the Gold Coast was enjoying prosperity, as there were good markets in Europe and elsewhere for cocoa and other crops grown by the people. Sometimes the farmers from the villages would come to the store with more money than they knew what to do with.

They would ask us to help them to choose gifts and clothing for their entire family. This meant buying presents for three generations of both sexes and of all ages. By the time we girls had done this the farmers came to the conclusion that we were very helpful people. A father or an uncle would propose to send a daughter or a niece from one of the villages to live with us and be trained. As a matter of fact we did take some of these girls into our home to give them a chance of being with us. But for lack of room we had to refuse many who wished to come. From the time I was nine years old it had been my hope that I might in some way serve the girls and women of Africa, wherever the need was greatest. So I never missed an opportunity for personal contact with them, either in our own home or in visiting.

" Later on my sister and I spent some months in England. Then we went to France, and on to our cousins in Senegal, French West Africa. We were able to compare the methods of colonial government used by the French and the English. Afterwards we returned to the Gold Coast, and I took a post as assistant secretary to the newly formed Gold Coast Agricultural Society, which had both African and European members. At this time plans were being made for the great college at Achimota. I realised that a new day was dawning for the education of Gold Coast boys and girls. I watched with breathless interest every new development. I was thrilled when I saw the foundations of the first buildings being laid. I watched with almost equal interest the new hospital for African patients.

" Quite suddenly my father had a severe breakdown and was ordered by the doctors to leave the Gold Coast for a long period. My sister and I went to take care of him. We took a flat near London, and made a home there for ourselves and two younger sisters who went to school in the neighbourhood. Our home became a centre for those of African race who visited London, whether they came from Africa proper or from the United States of North America or from the West Indies. People were beginning to recognise that the Negro had something to contribute to the world in music and in art.

" It was a great joy when my old friend Kathleen arrived in London with her husband Kamba Simango. She was a bright and beautiful girl with great artistic gifts. We had not seen each other since she left Africa with her aunt, Mrs. Casely Hayford, to raise money in America for an industrial school for girls in Freetown. Kathleen and I were one in our desire to help our sisters in Africa. She and her husband had pledged themselves for work in Portuguese East Africa among Kamba Simango's own people. He belonged to the Vandau tribe and was educated at Mount Selinda School and at Lovedale. Then he was sent to Hampton in Virginia, where Booker Washington was trained.[1] He finished his studies at Columbia University, New York.

" He and Kathleen were looking forward with eagerness to their life work. He went to Portugal to study the language of the colony in which he hoped to work. Kathleen remained in London. There she was seized with sudden illness and died in hospital. Her husband hastened to her, but

---

[1] See *Heroes of Health*, pp. 115–125.

arrived just too late to see her alive. Kathleen's death was not only a tragic loss to her own relations but to all of us who had the welfare of Africa and its women at heart.

" Kamba Simango returned to continue his studies in Portugal. In September, 1925, a month before he was due to sail for Africa, we were married in London. After a short time in Portugal we left for Angola, and spent eight months visiting mission stations there. This visit was a great help to us, as we started new work in the territory of the Mozambique in Portuguese East Africa on the other side of the continent.

" Apart from any other work my husband and I are doing here in Africa, I believe our home is of real value to the community. We try to live a natural Christian life with our children. They are just two healthy boys, full of high spirits and happy mischief. They get a great deal of fun out of every day, with their pets, their garden, and their little friends. Louis, the elder, speaks English and Chindau fluently, changing from one language to another with ease. David, not yet three years old, is more at home in Chindau.

" Our home is, as it were, set on a high hill for the community to watch. Anything they consider worth while they can try to copy. I hesitate to say that ours is an ideal home, but we try to make it the best we can attain. It is open for any of the community to visit. They know we are here to help or advise them at any time. Louis and David have always been the children of the community. In their own way they have helped us in what we are trying to teach. From their earliest days I have invited other mothers to come in and see how

I was trying to teach and train my little sons. The mothers have watched the happy relationship between us and our children. Sometimes they have been surprised that I could find time to play with them. Then the mothers have gone away and copied something they have seen or heard in our home.

" White friends of Africa have done self-sacrificing work in every part of the continent. They are doing it still. But I believe that it is by her own sons and daughters that Africa will really be won. For this reason I am happy to live here in this part of Africa, which is certainly very far away from my childhood's home and my own family. I have the sure knowledge that, however imperfectly, I am helping by sympathy, understanding, and love to contribute something worth while for the service of Africa."

PART III
PATHWAYS OF SERVICE

CHAPTER 9
TEACHING YOUNG AFRICA

I

A Great Fellowship

THE wise African wife and mother has always been something of a teacher and nurse in her own home, and she has established religion there. But in changing Africa there are many African girls who may never marry at all and others who postpone marriage for a few years that they may take up some definite calling. Widows and wives deserted by their husbands have to support and educate their children. Married women begin to find that without neglecting home they can do some teaching side by side with their husbands. This is especially the case as the children grow older and the mothers gain experience of life. African women begin to follow the women of the West.

The greatest fellowship of workers in every land is the fellowship of those who become teachers. They work in many languages and in all kinds of schools. But true teachers are always friends with one another. A lecturer on education in an English college went to Africa lately on a tour. When he came back he wrote a splendid book called *The School in the Bush*. He dedicated it to " the faithful village teachers in Africa."

Teachers learn a great deal from the history of education, for the whole past belongs to the whole fellowship. Some countries are only beginning to have schools, others have had them for hundreds of years. Centuries ago in Europe learning was

"EVERY WOMAN TEACHER COUNTS IN AFRICA"

only for a few, the people were untaught. Boys took long journeys in search of schools, little or no provision was made for girls. Does it not sound like Africa ? When education spread in Europe many mistakes were made. Teachers were often untrained, schools were short of supplies, classes were far too large, teaching had more to do with books and lessons than with life. The old mistakes made in Europe were repeated in Africa. But where Europe is slowly learning a better way, there is happily good hope that Africa will find a quicker way to truth.

The striking thing about the great fellowship of teachers in the West and in Africa is that its members keep on learning all the time. The best ones never hold out a certificate and say, " I know how to teach ; I am trained." The best teachers continue to be pupils, and when they get a holiday they often just begin to learn something more so that they may have more to give.

How can we make the African part of this great fellowship of teachers real to our minds ? Have you ever seen an airplane flying across the sky ? People in it can look down on towns and villages and kraals, and see human beings moving about like little ants. It would be rare fun to glide day after day over the whole continent of Africa, look-ing for schools. There would be enormous tracts of country with no schools at all. Great groups of buildings, like Achimota on the Gold Coast, or Lovedale in South Africa, would be seen here and there. There would be numbers of middle-sized buildings, and thousands upon thousands of little half-hidden school-houses scattered in the bush. Only when children pour out of them could any one guess they were schools. In most places there would be six or eight or even ten boys for every girl. Let the airplane circle a little till the teachers come out—what a huge fellowship ! For every little bush school is taught by an African or an African and his wife ; the larger schools have a staff part white, part African ; some schools have both men and women teachers ; others—not many yet—have women alone.

Every woman teacher counts in Africa. Multiply

the present number by ten and there would still be need for more. Africa is waiting for many things, but perhaps African women teachers are wanted most of all. The women who teach differ almost as much as the schools. Some have had years of training in a secondary school or college and hold high government certificates. Some, like Rachel Masinga, are head-mistresses of important schools, or members of a large teaching staff. Many, like Gracie Miyeni and the teachers in the island school (pp. 109, 111), have been trained for a mission certificate. Others who have done fine work, like Noma-mbotwe and Mariya (p. 110), have only learned to use their gifts by experience in a mission school. Wives who teach have often had only short or broken training while with their husbands at a " refresher " course.

Now we leave our airplane and come close up to some African women teachers at their work. RACHEL MASINGA, head-mistress of the Girls' Boarding School at Hope Fountain in Matabeleland, shall tell her story in her own words.

" I am a Zulu. I was born in 1895 at Umzumbe, a place on the sea-coast of Natal. I have never known any other religion than that of Jesus Christ. I went to a boarding-school near my home till I passed the sixth standard. I then went to Amanzimtoti, the great training institution in Natal, until I had taken my teacher's certificate. After that I was asked to take charge of the day school at Hope Fountain. I had to take five days' journey to get there. I believe I am the first Zulu woman teacher to come to Matabeleland.

" When I began work in the day school I had thirty children. Most of them could neither read

nor write. Then girls began to come and ask if
they might live with me and learn ; some of them
wanted to escape from bad marriages they were
being forced into at home. So in the year 1916
Mnali and I (Mnali is the name we call our missionary) thought we might start a boarding-school

"I AM RESPONSIBLE"

for girls. We sent notices round. The first year
we had only about six scholars, for the Matabele
do not think it is important to educate girls. We
all lived in two rooms in an out-building of Mnali's
house. From 1917 we have gone on increasing
every year ; we have forty-nine girls as I write.

" Our hostel is a large red-brick building facing Hope Fountain valley. When we had twenty girls it held us all, but soon another dormitory had to be built on the bank at the back. We show the girls that it is possible to live in a Native way and yet be clean and tidy. The whole day is carefully planned from six in the morning to the preparation of next day's lessons after supper at night. The girls, who vary in age from six to twenty, keep the house clean and tidy, tend the gardens and learn laundry work and needlework. Mnali's wife inspects the house and the girls' clothing once a week. On Friday and Saturday nights, as well as every afternoon, we have games, and the Saturday afternoon swim in the bathing pool is very jolly and noisy. The girls sing very well and give a concert every year in Buluwayo, which brings in quite a lot of money for the school.

" Government inspectors visit us every year and take great interest in our progress. As head-mistress I am responsible for order and the general arrangements in the school. I have for my assistant a Native of the Colony, trained at Lovedale. Our industrial mistress was trained at Tiger Kloof Institution. We have two pupil teachers who will, we hope, go from us to Tiger Kloof to complete their training. Two matrons look after the work of the hostel, the preparing of the food, and the comfort of the girls. This completes our family, except that Mnali, our missionary, must be included, for he is very fond of all his children and comes to see them every day.

" We are very ambitious. We want our Hope Fountain School to be the best in the country.

We believe that God will use it to raise the women of Matabeleland."

Since she wrote this story Rachel Masinga has married. Her good, capable husband is a teacher in another place and Rachel his wife works beside him earnestly and well.

II

MARIYA, GRACIE, AND CHRISTINA

Many African women teachers are beginning to shape their lives with a wise and steady purpose. A fine girl in a West African village passed all the standards in the local school. She saw how little was being done to help the community to rise to a better life. So she went first to the teachers' training class and then, to gain experience, went to teach for two years in a town school. After that she asked to be sent back to the school in her own village. For two years she worked happily and was a strong influence among her people. Then she married a schoolmaster in another village and at once became a leader among the girls in her new home.

Out on an island in Lake Nyasa, a few miles from Likoma, there is a school which has eighty girls on its roll. It is worked entirely by African women teachers. A white missionary visits them once a fortnight. Those teachers are real members of the great fellowship, they want to improve their work. During the week-ends they prepare busily by themselves for the second teachers' examination arranged by the mission. When the visiting missionary comes their work is marked and a little help is given.   The girls are being taught up to the preliminary standard of the women teachers' certificate.   Order and happiness are to be found in the school.

MARIYA belongs to an East African tribe well known for the vigour of its women.   Life at home had become too difficult for her.   She was betrothed to the son of a witch doctor, but finding he had already another wife she refused to marry him.   The witch doctor was so angry that he cursed her, saying she would never marry or bear a child.   She went to one of the large towns with a woman relation and was engaged to help a young white missionary in her day school.   She had a gift for teaching and before long the English girl and the African girl who worked together became friends.

Presently Mariya had to make a choice.   Her father wanted the cows and goats he would get for his daughter, so he pressed her to marry.   Just then some of the other teachers were getting married and Mariya felt a little lonely.   But the young white teacher was going for a year to England and Mariya felt she must stay herself to take charge of the school.   She did this with great success.

Another offer of marriage came, for the girl was capable and attractive.   But Mariya would not answer at once.   She wrote to her friend in England saying, " I want to see if we could have fellowship together, he and I and God."   Before long the man was sent to prison, so Mariya had been wise to wait.

Some time later she married and had a Christian wedding.   She continued her school work, teaching her girls and entering into the difficulties in their lives. When they left school they had to face temptations in the town. Some of the girls were drawn into evil ways before their wedding day. So Mariya started a league or society for girls who wanted to live a pure, clean life. It was called a torch-bearers' league, because each member was to be like a light or torch to other girls. Mariya made rules for the league, a meeting was held every week, and the girls paid a small monthly subscription. The money went to buy a wedding present for every member who on her marriage had a record of good life behind her. The league goes on still. There are others like it in Africa.

Mariya has a little daughter, who now goes to the young missionary's day school, and a baby son. She is a member of the Church committee and does useful work.

GRACIE MIYENI began life in the depths of misery, but when she died in 1931 she was surrounded by honour and love. Nearly forty years ago a son was born to a Swiss missionary in the Transvaal. In honour of this event, the chief gave him a cow and a calf and a little slave girl. Of course the child became free at once. But she was not an easy charge. The little creature had been starved. She devoured enormous plates of maize, she ate up all the food given to another little girl ; the family thought the house had become full of mice until they saw a little black figure creeping about at night hunting for food and eating up everything she could find. Her little body got fat while her arms and legs were still like sticks. But by the time she was eight years old Gracie was a charming, plump little girl.

In due time she went to be trained as a teacher

and after four years' study came back with her certificate. She was made a teacher in the school and did her work well. Before long she married a fellow-teacher—a Christian like herself—and they set up a happy home. But consumption laid hold of the young husband. Gracie worked bravely to carry on the school, care for her house and four children, and nurse her patient husband. He died.

For nine long years Gracie worked on, winning the respect of the whole community, white and black. Though temptations surrounded her as a young widow, she lived a blameless life. She continued to teach in the evening school, but in order to support her children she took daily sewing and washing. At her funeral one of the speakers was a young African teacher whom she had helped. He said, " Gracie Miyeni could go to meet God without fear."

A missionary from Scotland saw some of her school girls in Nyasaland turn into useful teachers. She has written the story of one of them for this book.

" Another of my pupils was CHRISTINA. She learned English very quickly and was a model both in and out of school. She was the first of my girls who seemed to be really in love with the man she was going to marry. From the very first they were lovers and friends. They have had a happy life now for more than twenty-five years.

" After her marriage Christina and her husband went as pioneer teachers to another country where they did, and are still doing, splendid work.

" Seven years later I met Christina again. I was living in her home village, and she came back to visit her old mother, bringing two children with

her. I was having a meeting with the women
when to my surprise and pleasure I found Christina
and her children there.

" I was talking to the women about feeding
infants and bringing up children. My remarks
were not very well received. The old women did
not agree with my views. ' Such talk is for white
women,' they said. ' Our customs are different.
Have we not always suckled our babies when they
cried, and gone on doing so till they were running
about and talking ?   And how can a child learn to
obey before the second teeth come ? '   I paused
for a moment and suddenly Christina sprang to
her feet. I can picture her still, as she drew herself up, her baby boy strapped on her back, a little
girl of four holding on to her dress. She said :

" ' Every word that the Dona [so they call a
white woman in Nyasaland] has said is true. I
know it and have proved it. I have seen how the
white people train their children. I have tried to
train mine in the same way.' Then she turned to
her little girl. ' Mary, run away home to Granny.
I do not wish you to stay here.' The child gave
her a loving look and went off obediently at once.
Then Christina looked round and said :

" ' How many of you have children of Mary's
size who obey quickly without asking questions ? '
The women looked astonished and no one spoke.
Then Christina went on, ' Mary obeys me and her
father because we began to teach her when she
was a baby. If your children are disobedient and
troublesome it is your own fault. I wash and
dress my children in the morning and feed them.
Then I lay the baby on a mat in the shade or on
the bed. I leave them in the care of a little maid

and I go to school to help my husband in his work.'

" I sat down thankfully, feeling that Christina was teaching better than I could teach. Her husband, who is now a minister of the Church, is a man of fine character, but I think that Christina's character is even stronger and she has been a great influence in his life."

III

A TEACHER IN TRAINING SPEAKS

Many girl readers of this chapter will enter the great fellowship of teachers. One may set her heart on joining the staff of an advanced school or college, another may look forward to teaching in a day school in town, a third may go to work in the villages. But every modern African girl teacher will certainly wish to be trained. Perhaps she can take a full course and gain a good government certificate. Or she may have to rest content with simpler training than that.

During her training she will gain a great deal of knowledge. Knowledge has real value and is worth all it costs in hard work. But those who have read attentively the stories in this book will never believe that a girl who only piles up knowledge, studies the theory of education, or is familiar with the government code, has got everything a good teacher needs. There are bigger and deeper things which some of the wise, loving, half-trained teachers had, and which some of the fully trained ones may miss.

In every country, as well as in Africa, schools

suffer from the mistake of teachers who keep their lessons separate from life. Some years ago a school teacher in England offered to go out to teach in an African school. She had good certificates and could teach all the subjects in the time-table. But out of school hours she took no interest

A TEACHER IN TRAINING

in the children. She "wished to live her own life." To her, girls were like little hollow boxes into which knowledge had to be crammed. She did not think of them as living growing creatures to be helped towards beautiful lives. When she heard the kind of work a good teacher did in Africa she went hastily away.

In a little country school in the Southern States

of America a visitor found a worried Negro woman trying to make her unhappy little pupils repeat the boundaries and capital towns of all the United States and a long list of dates in history. A few miles away, in another school, a young Negro teacher trained at Hampton Institute was giving a lesson to children who were too interested even to look round when strangers came in. The teacher had pictures of a lion, a goat, and a cow. One child wrote the names of the animals on the blackboard. The others read the names. A sentence or two about each of them was made up by the children, written on the board, and eagerly read. They discussed where lions lived; a boy found the places on a map on the wall. Some stories about lions were promised for another day. The children told the teacher about the goats and cows in the village. They counted up their number and wrote it on the blackboard. A big friendly dog pushed the door open and came in. He put his cold nose on the hand of a startled child. The teacher led the merry laughter and coaxed the dog to stand at her side while she gave a lesson on kindness to animals. The children felt it was like a lovely game as they came up one by one to pat the big dog's head gently. But they had been learning reading, writing, arithmetic, and a little geography too, and the village animals had a better time because that lesson had been given.

Some of the girls at African training centres know English quite well and they are reading the new books written for young African teachers.[1]

[1] Such as *The Village Teachers' Guide*. London : S.P.C.K. By the staff of the Jeanes School, Kabete, Kenya. And *The Principles of Education for African Teachers in Training*, by Harold Jowitt. (Longmans.)

They are thinking about the real meaning of their work. If one of these teachers in training could come to talk to us about what she is learning, she would perhaps say something like this :

" We learn to think a lot about the child. Everything it does, as its little body grows and its little mind wakes up, tells the teacher something she ought to know. Each child is a separate person with a character and a life of its own. No one knows what a child will become when it grows up. That must be true, for Dr. Livingstone and Dr. Aggrey were only ordinary little boys and their mothers were ordinary little girls. There are stories in *Daughters of Africa* of unpromising children who became fine women. We teachers specially need to understand that the little girls we teach are getting ready in body and mind to bear children and have homes of their own. We can help them to be modest and pure. And we can help their mothers to shield them from evil. If there are tribal customs hurtful to girls we can try to get them changed.

" The children come to us from homes. They bring from there good things and bad. We have to try to build on what is good and to save them from what is evil. Love is our hope of doing this. In school we soon love each other. But love in the home matters more. The new ways learned at school, and all the changes in Africa, sometimes come between girls and their homes. But the love of parents and children for each other is like a bridge over a river in flood. Daughters by the bridge of love can enter into the life of home ; parents can pass over it to enter into the life of the school. Across that bridge, too, the teacher can pass. When she and the mothers of her children work together there will always be a welcome for her in the tribe. It is really a good thing that that teacher who saw nothing outside her schoolroom was not sent to Africa.

" In Africa we can never forget that all the homes make one great community ; ancient custom binds the clan or tribe together. We Africans are very proud of this. We want our schools to strengthen community life. We are sad when in towns and other places it is broken. Something is needed there to take its place. Many Africans are finding that the Christian Church can help. We teachers must honour this common life and teach our children to follow the good in its laws. Some girls will be mothers of future councillors and chiefs. When we try to teach good manners in school we can remind them that old Africa had good manners which are not out of date.

" How happy we shall be if we can make our school a centre of community life ! A proper country school has to do with making the village cleaner, the water purer, the food more nourishing, the fields and gardens more fertile, the cattle richer in increase, the chickens and eggs more abundant, the markets more profitable than before. When disease threatens the people, the school with its teacher and pupils can lead in the great battle for public health. We all know that Africa needs highly educated men and women of her various races who can follow professions or go into large business. Africa also needs highly trained artisans, medical workers, and nurses. But the most important groups in building up strong national life in Africa, as in other lands, will be the big communities of enlightened and well-educated village people.

"There was a time when education began to separate us from African customs and thought and made little of the beauty of African things. We even gave up our African names and took those of people in England. That day has gone. We are learning to make much of African languages in our teaching, for no strange speech can be like our mother's tongue. We want to make our schools rich with African art and music. We mean to tell African stories, ask African riddles, play African games. Folk tales can be collected in the holidays. In the great college at Achimota on the Gold Coast all these African things are sought. Love of laughter and love of beauty go together and we teachers want our schools to be as full of fun as of work. That an African child is meant to be merry is shown by its smiling face.

" Our school may not be near any great mountain, lake, or forest, but there is beauty wherever there is life. If the teacher's eyes are open to see it the children will see it too. We want them to feel that beauty has its place in school. We were once told a story from England which some of us will never forget. There was a show of drawings done by school children, not copies of other peoples' pictures but drawings in which the children tried to express what they saw and felt. The most beautiful of all were rough, unfinished drawings sent from a school in a town full of mills and factories, where children lived in narrow streets with high houses, and saw few trees or flowers. Their teacher taught them to watch the changing colour in the sky, and the rays of light which fell on the wet streets and sloping roofs after rain. The beauty appealed to the children and they drew what they saw. Men and women whose eyes were not opened saw only dismal, dirty streets.

" The best kind of beauty, of course, is the beauty of goodness and truth. There is evidence in *Daughters of Africa* that our country has a treasure of this. And fresh treasures have come to us in the Christian faith. Some people try to teach this beauty by words ; we begin to understand that it can only be taught by life. Someone good and true and loving is a text-book which children quickly read. You see, the character of the teacher makes its mark on the children, and the character of the children influences the home. Then the home touches the village, the village touches the tribe, and the tribe touches Africa. We young teachers sometimes feel small and frightened when we think of these things. And perhaps we shall be lonely when we face them in our future schools. But we are glad to belong to the great world-wide fellowship of teachers, who are all together learning how to be good and how to do good work."

CHAPTER 10

MINISTERS OF HEALTH

I

How it All Came to Pass

STORIES of Ada and of Kagei show how much women in old Africa had to do with battles against disease. Some of them had knowledge of herbs but most of them depended on magic. In the homes mothers tried with aching hearts to care for their sick and suffering children, calling the spirits to their aid. Ignorant treatment often did more harm than good.

But a new ministry of health was coming to Africa. It began far away in the lands of the West.

Long ago mothers in western lands were almost as ignorant as those in Africa, and those who nursed the sick knew little of what to do. But the heroes of health whose stories have been written for Africans,[1] were finding out about disease and nurses were being taught to care for the sick.

It took several years of hard preparation to learn to be a nurse. The English girls had to learn first how to scrub and clean the places where the sick

---

[1] *Heroes of Health.* See notice at front of book.

people were, how to clear away all that was unclean or unpleasant, how to wash those who were ill and make their beds, and even how to prepare for burial the bodies of those who died. After this came things that were more interesting, such as taking temperatures, keeping charts, observing changes in the patient, preparing and giving medicine and helping the doctor when an operation was being done. Most of the nurses learned also how to do maternity work. Numbers of mothers and babies who would have died were saved by their care and skill.

After a time every western country had a number of trained nurses ready to care for the sick. And in the hospitals some of the cleverest nurses were helping the doctors to train new nurses for their work. Then there came a day when doctors and nurses began to think about sick people of other races. They heard a call in their hearts to go to Asia and Africa and other parts of the world. The new day for Africa began when white doctors— some of them women—and white nurses came to the country as ministers of health. Many of these were missionaries. Some of them died in Africa, gladly giving their lives in exchange for the hundreds of lives they saved.

But something even greater came to pass. Africans themselves began to be ministers of health. At first only men would go to help ; women were too timid and shy. But by degrees they gained courage, and went to be trained like girls in western lands.

The discipline of hard work was not easy. Some found it difficult to be accurate, punctual, obedient, and to remember what they were told.

Some learned how to treat symptoms but forgot to watch how the patient was. Some were afraid of responsibility and could not rise to meet a sudden call, or got tired and gave up. Others had to be sent away because they were not worthy of trust, or fell under moral temptation. Some were hindered by old beliefs that illness came because the patient deserved it or had been bewitched.

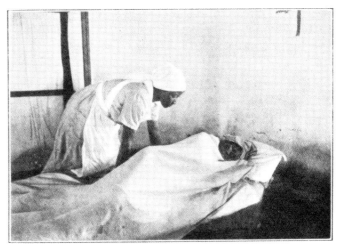

A YORUBA NURSE OBSERVING HER PATIENT

But many African girls persevered and learned to be good, capable, unselfish nurses. They are doing splendid service among their own people. Some are serving in hospitals or large centres, others are working almost alone in a distant country place. Some are employed by the Government, as in the Maternity and Child Welfare Clinic at Dar-es-Salaam where trained African nurses help. Everything is done with scientific skill, but so simply that the people can copy it in their own homes. The clinic is training African girls to go out for maternity work among their own people. In other cases town authorities employ trained African nurses. Many are working with the missionaries either in hospitals or in welfare work.

Some African trained nurses only give full-time service for a few years. Then, according to the custom of the country, they marry. But here and there an African nurse feels she is called, like the white woman, to remain unmarried that she may give herself entirely to her chosen work.

II

AFRICAN NURSES AT WORK

African nurses gain their training in various ways. A few have crossed the seas to Europe or America, seeking a certificate in a western hospital. This course is costly, and unfortunately openings in western hospitals are not easily found. But the wider experience is of advantage for those who want to train other nurses in Africa, or to go into private practice with a doctor there. In Africa itself opportunities for high-grade nursing training are increasing. This is the case both in government and in mission hospitals. In place after place doctors and nurses from many western lands are giving careful training to African women in little groups of four or five, or in larger parties of twenty or thirty. African girls of the best type are needed to be trained at such centres. In a few cases where white and African students have sat for the same examination for a certificate, the

African nurses have done well. When they go out to work after training, their character and capacity may pass through a searching test. The story of Brave Nurse Grace shows this.

In Chapter 5 we heard of the changes in the life of one place in the course of thirty years. Among the pupils in the college there was a Zulu girl, whom we will call GRACE.

Having passed through all the school standards, Grace decided to be a nurse. There was a little hospital close by with a certificated African nurse in charge. Grace went through her full hospital training and sat at Durban for her final nurses' examination with sixteen European candidates. She came out third.

Where was her professional work to be done? In a big hospital with long wards and plenty of doctors and other nurses always at hand? Not so. She found herself in a Native reserve in a country district about twelve miles from Durban. There, next door to the missionary and his wife, she had a tiny wood and iron hospital with two wards which could take in six patients. Besides that she had the whole district to visit and work in, and one bedroom in the hospital for her very own.

In the four years since Nurse Grace went to the little hospital she has had 1,117 out-patients and 112 in-patients in the wards. When cases are too difficult she can call in a doctor. Hers is a busy life. She is up by 5.30 in the morning. The usual daily business of a well-trained nurse has to be put through. That means washing the patients in the wards, making their beds, sweeping and dusting everything. The patients' breakfast comes—porridge and milk, with tea and bread if they are well enough. By this time the out-patients begin to arrive. Then if the day is fine the patients in the wards are moved on to the veranda. More out-patients gather and nurse attends to them. Up comes a messenger from the district that someone is very ill—nurse must come at once. The messenger waits to take her and will bring her back again. Sometimes the call is to perfect strangers and comes in the middle of the night. But nurse is never afraid. No one would hurt her, she says. Here is the story of one case to which Grace went not long ago :

" A few days ago," writes the missionary's wife, " Grace came to tell me that two heathen women had come to get her for a maternity case some miles away. They had been trying to help the mother themselves but had failed. It was then just after nine o'clock in the morning. Thirteen hours later, at 10.30 at night, nurse rapped at my window, asking me to telephone for the doctor at once. Four men were carrying the poor patient into the hospital on a stretcher made of a few branches. They had started at four in the after-noon, and nurse had hurried on ahead to get ready for the doctor and the patient. She had walked over fourteen miles and had had no food all day. But her only thought was for the patient. The poor woman arrived before midnight, having been carried for seven and a half hours on a hard stretcher, all the time in pain.

" The doctor came soon after. If you had looked into the dining-room of the mission house three hours later—in the very middle of the night —you would have seen the doctor enjoying a cup of hot cocoa and some food after a hard fight to save life. It was half-past four in the morning before nurse lay down for her night's rest, and she was up again at 6.30 ready to carry on. She was full of real joy and thankfulness because her patient's baby had been born alive."

The Isoko tribe live in a swampy district in West Africa in the delta of the Niger. In the wet season the country is all under water and the villages on higher ground stand like little islands in a lake. Once the Isoko tribe were apart from the rest of the world. In the last thirty years the four influences which have changed all Africa have brought changes to them—you will remember that these are trade, government, education, and a new religion.

Christianity was brought by a woman named RACHEL BRIBINA, who married an Isoko chief. She could not even read but she taught her husband and two other men about the God of Truth. When many people became Christians their neighbours were unkind to them, so they moved to a little village which they called Bethel.

In the year 1930 the first white missionary nurse came to live among Isoko women. There was no money to pay for a hospital, she had to work just where she could, going to and fro in the district. Soon she began to train some of the capable Isoko women to work with her. The maternity and welfare classes in which she taught them had splendid results. Bribina was one of the first pupils. She was so easy to teach. After three months she went with another member of the class to an outlying village where she welcomes to her home women who are in need. The quiet, dignified, shy woman is honoured through the whole district. Her patients say, " Her words are sweet to us." Her daughter Rebecca is the one well-educated Isoko girl. Her mother sent her to school, where she passed the sixth standard and took the first part of her pupil teachers' examination. Then she came to be interpreter for the missionaries. But nursing attracted her most of all. She took care of the mothers and babies. She saw to the cleaning of the dispensary and the welfare centre. She could even take a maternity case if the older nurses were not free.

Another early pupil was SARAH IKEPOSI, who used to be a busy midwife before the white nurse came. She was clever and was often called out to other villages, though she only knew old African ways. Would Sarah be angry and feel she could make money no longer because the white nurse had come ? Sarah was too fine a woman to look on the new work as a rival. It was better than her own and she welcomed it. Soon she might be seen literally dragging her patients to be patients of the new white nurse. With generous nature and large heart Sarah used her little mud hut as a home for women waiting for the birth of a child. It was a fresh test for Sarah when Rebecca, Bribina's daughter, came, young and eager, full of modern ways of work ; Sarah was only used to the ways of the bush. But she quietly took Rebecca as her example and teacher. Cleanliness in person and in method soon became a mark of Sarah's work.

Sarah still practises as a midwife, but she takes no payment from her patients. She looks on every case as a call from God. With her long experience and new knowledge she has become a most useful citizen. She is welcome everywhere, with her affectionate nature and cheery smile.

A third member of that first maternity class in Bethel was MARY ABOYE, a grey-haired widow. She had long been practising in a large town on the edge of the district, where the people were wild, strong-minded, and obstinate. But Mary was a born leader. Even after she became a Christian she exercised a strong influence in the town and held the admiration of the people. In the midwifery class Mary proved so intelligent that she was kept for three months' special training. She had charge of the welfare centre. She adopted new methods quite quickly and became a competent midwife. Her great aim was to fit herself for work in her own town. But her strong character marked her out for pioneer work. Would she be willing to go to open a maternity home in a new place? It was responsible work. " If God calls, how can I refuse? " said Mary, and she went. For three months she worked till the new centre was established. Then she went back to her own town, where she had been sorely missed. The townspeople have built her a small maternity home, where she lives and devotes her time to the work.

III

THE STORY OF AGIRI UJA

" I am sorry, but I cannot accept you for training." As the wife of the white doctor in Uganda said this, disappointment like a cloud covered the face of the tall, vigorous African girl who stood before her. " You see," went on the speaker, " I am only just beginning to take African girls to train as midwives. The population of Uganda is getting smaller because so many mothers and babies die. The Government and the mission want to send out fully trained midwives through the land. Though all the teaching will be given in their own language the pupils must be able to read and write, they must also know some arithmetic. Now you," the doctor's wife continued very kindly, " can only read badly, you can scarcely write, and you know no arithmetic. You would not understand the lessons given to the young nurses. You could not take notes as they have to do."

Then the doctor's wife, herself a hospital sister who had trained many hospital nurses in England, saw that this frank, eager African girl was full of purpose. Her clear, steady eyes, her upright bearing, her courage under heavy disappointment gave promise for the future.

" If you like to learn to read and write and do sums you can come back to me at the end of three months. If you know enough then I will accept you." The white nurse knew that this was a real test. For her visitor, AGIRI UJA, was over twenty years of age. And she could only get the knowledge she needed by sitting in a class with quite little girls who were learning to read and write.

Happily the African girl was made of splendid stuff. It was no passing fancy which made her want to be a nurse. The purpose had been growing for years. Her father was a man of good position in the island of Buvuma, in the Victoria Nyanza, the largest of all the great inland seas of Africa. Sleeping sickness became so terribly bad

AGIRI UJA—LEADER IN A SPLENDID WORK

that all the people were removed by the government from this island and several others, to the mainland.[1] There, in Kyagwe, Agiri's family settled. She went to the small mission school and began to learn a little. She became a Christian.

News reached her that other girls like herself were going to be trained as nurses. She knew it was something big and worth while. She asked her father if she might go. He promptly refused. She did not know enough herself to explain what nursing was. He thought she wanted to take care of children in a white family. But Agiri kept the purpose in her heart.

One day a girl came to stay in the village who knew about the new nursing work. It was an honourable calling, she said. Several chiefs had sent their daughters to be trained as midwives. Among others the great Katikiro, Sir Apolo Kagwa, had sent his daughter Susanna to learn. Then Agiri's parents gave her leave to go and see the white trained nurse who, with her husband the doctor, was doing so much for the women of Uganda. Poor Agiri! With all this story behind her offer, it was a big test to be sent back to learn to read and write.

But the girl had patience as well as purpose. She went back to the small school in her village and took her place in a class of little girls. The missionary wondered at her courage as she worked away, never turning aside. At the end of three months, she came back to the head of the Training School and was admitted as a student. And now Agiri Uja, who once applied and was refused, has not only finished her training but is the foremost

[1] The story is told in *Heroes of Health*, pp. 103-109.

of all the African midwives in Uganda and leader in a splendid work.

The final examination which she and the other African girls had to pass is equal to that which the Central Board of Midwives in England requires before maternity nurses are allowed to practice. So in Uganda mother and baby can have care as skilful as that given in any English home.

The work, which has its headquarters in the beautiful central Maternity Training School in the capital of Uganda, spread out through the protectorate. In February, 1931, eleven years later, Princess Alice, a grand-daughter of Queen Victoria of England, came to open the new women's hospital and maternity centre at a place called Mukono. She was told that thirty maternity and child welfare centres had been opened in various districts, that over two thousand women had been attended at child-birth, and that ninety-five capable African girls had passed the government examination which made them qualified midwives. " It is a healthy and encouraging sign," she said, " that so many of your better educated girls are coming forward to take up the noble profession of nursing."

Agiri was at the heart of this advance. She was sent to take charge of a country centre over a hundred miles from the Training School. The people were difficult, but they soon learned to love her and she won them to healthy ways. After a time a practising school where students could get experience in their work was opened not far from the central training school. Agiri was put in charge.

It was a great day when the practising school was opened in 1925. Many Europeans were present and over two thousand Africans. The figures that interest us most are two attractive women in the centre of the scene. One is the first African woman in the land, the Lady Irene, wife of His Highness Sir Daudi Chwa, Kabaka of Uganda. The other is the young head midwife, Agiri herself. The Lady Irene speaks of all that the maternity workers have done for Uganda, and of the self-sacrificing service of the white doctor and his wife. Then Agiri, in her graceful nurse's dress steps forward, kneels, and presents the Lady Irene with a silver-gilt key on a purple cushion. In a moment the door is open and the visitors stream into the well-fitted building with its two wards for African mothers.

There we leave Agiri, a daughter of whom Africa may be proud, a steadfast, loyal, capable woman, full of humility and love. She might more than once have married and had a home of her own. But the purpose that began long ago in Kyagwe still rules her life.

Two brief stories show still more what this trained maternity work has meant:

At Iganga, a place in Uganda, there was a little hospital and maternity centre under the charge of an English missionary. In 1929 she had to spend a year in England and no white woman could go to take her place. So two of the certified African midwives were sent down from the great hospital at Mengo and put in charge. The maternity work grew four times as large while they had it in their hands. Their care of the mothers and babies was so loving that when the year was over the local chiefs did not want to lose their aid. They signed a letter asking that even when the English missionary came back the two African midwives might remain with them still.

The fame of the maternity training in Uganda spread through Africa. Students were sent up from Tanganyika to be trained. The governor's wife came from Kenya to see the work and had students from Uganda sent to help her to begin a work like it. Officials from Nigeria, the Sudan, and other places, came to see what was being done.

AT THE OPENING OF "THE HOUSE OF BIRTH"

Far to the south-east the news spread to an important mission station in Tanganyika Territory where mothers mourned the constant loss of their babies. The group of Christians, some of those belonging to the great diocese of Zanzibar, talked things over and resolved to take action, bearing the cost themselves. They built a two-roomed, whitewashed house, with a thatched roof, and called it in their own tongue "The House of Birth." The beds, basins, water pots, and mats were all presents from the people. When the house was opened, about a year ago, with a service of blessing, there in the veranda stood a smiling row of African nurses, all mothers themselves. They were not then " qualified " like Grace or Agiri (see pp. 125, 133). But the white sister in the hospital near by taught the new customs at the House of Birth. The nurses promised to use them faithfully. The crowd who collected were told that the House of Birth was opened to save their babies and that every mother could come and claim her place. Then the men were invited to come in to examine everything and give approval if they would. Meantime the women stood in groups and talked eagerly of babies already saved and of other mothers who were coming to have babies born safely in the House of Birth. That very night a heathen woman was brought in. The African nurses cared for her and the white nurse stood by in case of need. Even the conservative old grandmothers are glad now about the opening of the House of Birth.

Ever since then the African nurses have been studying and now eighteen of them are qualified midwives, some having the government certificate. They are led by the wife of the African clergyman, who has been foremost in allowing his wife to be called out at night to attend to mothers and their babies.

CHAPTER 11

SOCIAL SERVICE

I

THE STORIES OF CHARLOTTE MAXEKE AND GEORGIA WASHINGTON

ONE of these women lives in South Africa, the other lives in the United States of America. Their work differs widely. Both are drawing towards the close of long and active lives.

The story of CHARLOTTE MANYE MAXEKE'S work has come from men and women of her own race, from English and American people who have worked with her in Johannesburg, and from newspapers in South Africa. Now that she has given up public office it is possible to see her life-work as a whole.

She is of Bantu stock on her father's side, her mother belonged to the Xosa tribe. Her father became a Christian, so she began her education in mission schools. Her lovely deep voice gained her a welcome as a concert singer in Kimberley. Afterwards she was taken with a group of young African singers to Great Britain. Charlotte Manye had the honour of singing before Queen Victoria. Two years later another trip was arranged for the singers. This time they travelled farther, going on to Canada and the United States.

During her stay in America, Charlotte was offered a college education. She eagerly accepted the chance. She was sent to Wilberforce University, in Cleveland, Ohio. Here she made friends with some of the future leaders among Negroes in the United States. She did her college work with steady purpose and often lectured in America on the needs of her people at home.

Thirty years ago (in 1901) she returned to South Africa. She began active pioneer work in the African Methodist Episcopal Church. A couple of years later an African student named M. M. Maxeke, who had been with her at Wilberforce College, came back as an ordained man ready to be a minister among his own people. He and Charlotte Manye were married and lived in happy fellowship for many years.

In one school after another husband and wife did good work for their Church. Then a call came which was a direct preparation for Charlotte Maxeke's future work. The Paramount Chief of the Tembu tribe opened a private school. He invited the Maxekes to come and take charge of it. But their work was far wider than the classrooms. Mrs. Maxeke was drawn into the life of the tribe. She took a full place in their councils. She often spoke in the court of the chief.

After a time, owing to failure of health, the husband and wife moved into Johannesburg. There Charlotte Maxeke soon became a leader in church work and social service. She was president of the missionary association. She was a strong advocate of temperance. Her gift of eloquence, whether in English or in the languages of the Zulu and Basuto tribes, made her a popular speaker everywhere. In later life she spoke—and spoke well—on the same platform as Queen Victoria's grand-daughter, the Princess Alice.

Charlotte Maxeke was the founder of the Bantu Women's League, which was formed to protect the rights of African women. It has stirred a wider public spirit among them.

Her largest service began after her husband's death. The town authorities, knowing the need for her wise and womanly service, appointed her Native Probation Officer to the Magistrates' Court in Johannesburg. She was given an office where she could meet and deal with the girls and women brought before the court. The magistrates and law officials knew and trusted her. So did all the Native men and women for miles around. Her knowledge of them and of their lives enabled her to act on their behalf. She found now the value of her work in the councils of the Tembu chief. She was wise enough to see where justice lay in the cases that were being tried in the Magistrates' Court. But her fulness of love and pity made her the friend of the poorest and most degraded women, the guardian of each neglected or outcast child. She visited the four women's prisons and could influence the prisoners, many of whom had been arrested for illegal brewing, others for using a knife in some drinking quarrel. She found work for the women who had finished their sentence, and cared for prisoners' children while their mothers were in gaol. When cases of difficulty between husbands and wives were brought into court, Mrs. Maxeke was able to act as advisor and friend. She was not content with seeking to help the prisoners, she worked steadily to remove the causes of crime.

This African woman, with her keen sense of humour, her sane judgment, and her kindly heart, no longer holds public office. But she remains, as Professor Jabavu of the South African Native College at Fort Hare said, " One of the great figures of Bantu progressive life and one of the best known figures in public life in South Africa."

The story of GEORGIA WASHINGTON shows what a woman of African race can do to uplift the life of village people in the Western land to which her forefathers were taken as slaves.

In Alabama, one of the Southern States of North America, at a village called Mount Meigs, there is a group of buildings known as the People's Village School. In front of a fringe of pine trees stands the two-story school-house. Near by is the teachers' house, the domestic science building, a small workshop, and a boys' cottage. The school owns a number of chickens and pigs, one mule, three cows, and twenty-seven acres of land.

Not far off is the village, like many others in the district, except that the houses are better built. The whole place has an air of health and quiet welfare. Ask a villager what has brought this true prosperity. He will tell you it is largely the People's Village School. He may add that pupils from it have gone on to other schools and then out into the world as doctors, dentists, nurses, farmers, instructors in farm work and home work, school teachers, and even pastors.

As we look at the buildings with respect and interest, the boys and girls—some 250 of them— flock out, laughing and playing as they come. School is over for the day. And here, with both hands held out to welcome her visitors, comes a little dark-faced, white-haired woman. It is Georgia Washington herself, the founder and

GEORGIA WASHINGTON RECEIVING SCHOOL FEES

principal of the school. Her work and her story should be as well known in Africa as they are in the United States.

Her parents were slaves. When she was a little girl her father and brother were sold to a new master, while she and the smaller children were left with their mother. When the war which freed the slaves was over, the family were united again. Georgia remembers being carried on the back of an old man to the place where her father was. It was a joyful meeting.

Then began a time of hard work and poor living. The father got a little piece of land to farm. On it he tried to support his wife and their ten children. But there was not food enough for all. So the mother went to earn money by cooking for white people ; little Georgia stayed at home to care for the children and the house. In spare moments she learned to read. At last, when she was fourteen, she got to school for seven months. Oh ! how hard she worked ! At last her teacher arranged to send her to Hampton Institute, the great school opened for Negroes after the war.

While at Hampton Georgia had free instruction, but she had to pay for her board. She earned money for this by cleaning rooms, washing dishes, and doing laundry work. Five years later she was made a helper and served on the Hampton staff for ten years more. Then the call to her life-work came.

The great Negro leader, Booker Washington, had gone down from Hampton to Tuskegee in Alabama. He wanted to see a new school in a neglected district. So he wrote to Hampton inviting Georgia Washington to come and do this work. That was nearly forty years ago and she has been there ever since.

It was rough work at first. There was no place for the young teacher to live in. The neighbours gave her a meal in turns. She began her school in a little rented cabin ; four small boys came to be taught.

The Negro community lived in one-room log huts, with a tiny kitchen attached. They thought little of cleanliness or order for their children or themselves. But the teacher soon changed that. Before long no scholars dare come to school in the morning with untidy hair, uncleaned shoes, or with buttons missing off their clothes. Dirty pupils were promptly sent home to come back as soon as they were clean.

The People's Village School became the centre of the whole community. Year after year the teacher talked to the men about their work, till some of them bought bits of land and began to go to the Farmers' Conference at Tuskegee to learn how to cultivate it well. In that district Negro farmers now own 3,000 acres of land. In time they built nice houses with five or six rooms and separate sleeping places for boys and girls. The houses had real windows too.

The mothers also gathered round the school. They were taught simple housekeeping, cooking, and sewing. They learned how to cook and pre-serve food. The teacher talked to them about the proper care of children. At first some of the parents did not see the good of the new ways and tried to stick to the bad old ones. But they found that when teacher once said a thing she would not change. So one after another they agreed to what she wished.

Right out into the district her influence went. For some years she has had an " opportunity school " every summer for elder men and women who have never before had a chance to learn. Early in the morning they may be seen hastening along the high road to school with their books under their arms.

The usual school subjects are taught in the classrooms, of course, and all that prepares the children to be good home-makers. But they learn, too, to serve the whole community. In their clubs and games they are taught to think of others. Groups of boys and of girls go to outlying places to clean up rooms, tend the sick, read the Bible to the ignorant, and do all kinds of simple social service. Once a year there is a great community play day, when children from all the neighbouring districts gather at the school and have a glorious time.

What a story of success ! Yes, but it is a story of struggle and sacrifice too. The little teacher has often been tired and the school has always been poor. Times have been bad and money has been scarce. But years and difficulties have not broken Georgia Washington's faith and hope. The children and their parents stand by and help. Here is part of a letter which shows how the school fees are paid. " Three of my boys," writes Georgia Washington, " hauled two loads of wood to pay for their schooling, and brought also a package of pea-nuts. Another small boy said his mother had a turkey for me, but he could not bring it, so I shall send for it. Another mother sent me a lot of good nuts to pay fees for her four children. A pound of butter came for three children, and one parent sent twenty-five pounds of beef for two children. Thus we are keeping on."

Other parents, whose children were being educated and who had no money for fees, gave hay for the mule, the loan of a cow to give the teacher milk, and a hen to lay eggs. One man built a coal shed for the school and secured free education for his family.

II

Some Shorter Tales

All over Africa, in large towns and in country parts, training in social services goes quietly on. In Johannesburg, for instance, splendid work is being done in the Bantu Social Centre and in all the work linked with the Bridgman Memorial Hospital. Here missionaries and their white fellow-workers are busied in lifting up the downtrodden and setting men and women on their feet. Linked with them are Africans who follow in the pathway of service. The hospital besides tending the sick, trains young African nurses. The Helping Hands Club not only shelters and finds wholesome work for hundreds of Bantu girls, it provides training for those who want to learn to serve. There are quiet centres of purity and hope, like that known as Ekatuleni, where white women pour out the rich treasure of their own life and gather women of Africa into a true fellowship of loving social service.

Some African social workers have been long at their posts. One such is Sister Nannie, who works for the Dutch Reformed Church. A native of Mozambique, she came to the Cape many years ago. She has given her life to serve girls who have no home, or work, or money, and are in peril on the streets. She has two little rooms in which she can shelter them. There many little dark babies have made a sad beginning of life. But how much sadder it would have been without Sister Nannie to befriend the young mother and her child.

Other African social workers after a time of training have begun their work. Some years ago two African girls, who had been educated at well-know mission schools, came to England on their way to take training in social work in the United States. Both were Christians ; one was a Fingo, the other a Zulu. They stayed in the house of English friends, making many happy links which will never be broken. They went on to America, and finally returned to their own land. One of them—the Fingo—is helping to train teachers at Lovedale, who will do social work through their schools. The other—the Zulu—has gone back to her own people and is working in the villages of her tribe. She is seeking to band young people into clubs, and to lead girls, and boys too, into lives of purity and service for others. Their friends in America and in England follow their work with sympathy and hope.

In Africa, as in Western lands, girls are being brought face to face with social duty while still at school. The Girl Guides of the West and the Wayfarers of Africa are learning great lessons for life. Thousands of African Wayfarers are being trained through this organisation in habits of cleanliness, health, truth, and purity. And they are learning to use their powers in the service of others. For behind the adventure of Wayfarers' doings are many African teachers who welcome the chance of starting their pupils in unselfish service at the 'outset of life.

ANN DAOMA, who closed her long life of active service in the opening days of 1932, will long be remembered in Cape Town. One of Africa's heroic missionaries—Bishop Mackenzie—found her on the roadside by her dying mother. Slave-traders had left them there as mere useless things. Ann was so small that the Bishop often carried her on his shoulder through the wild country. She was sent to a mission school and was a quick learner. Being a good manager and able to control others, it was believed that her father must have been a chief. After a time she was given charge of the infants in the school and kept this post till 1919, when she retired on a small government pension.

For more than sixty years Ann was a familiar figure in Cape Town, working among the children and the sick and poor. Everyone knew her and her work. A stranger to the city wanted one day to go to the school where she lived. He gave the cabdriver the address. The driver said he did not know the place. The stranger explained. At last the man's face lit up. " Oh, you mean Miss Ann's Home," he said, and drove there at once. The gentle little woman went freely into slums in Cape Town where no policeman would go alone. Quiet and kindly as she was, she could give a firm rebuke. Two young sailors stopped her in the street, asking the way to a certain house. Ann said she was sorry, but she had never heard of the place. They said, " Of course you know it," and told her it was an evil house. Ann, moved with indignation, said, " How can you, who are English gentlemen, ask a black woman such a thing ? Think of your mothers and go back to your ship." The boys looked ashamed and turned back the way they came.

Ann loved everything beautiful, especially the country and open-air life. She is buried in the beautiful cemetery at Cape Town, beside two white friends whom she had loved all her life.

We have written of social service in the Union of South Africa. But West Africa must also find place.

In Western lands many women whose husbands are merchants or professional men, give time gladly to social service. This voluntary work is also attractive to African women of the same class.

In one of the large West African ports two women stand out among the rest. Their father was a wealthy trader and one of the first who became a Christian. One of the daughters, a trained maternity nurse, has a school with over 150 pupils. Her girls get a good education and sound training for life. The other, whose husband is a doctor, takes active part in trying to keep the streets of the town free from vice and in securing proper conditions for girls engaged in office work. She interests the women of the Church in social questions and calls on them for aid. When necessary she approaches the pastors, or the bishop, or even the government authorities. She takes pains to understand the questions she deals with and is not afraid to speak her mind.

III

SOCIAL TRAINING OVERSEAS AND IN AFRICA

How cheerful it looked as we drove up to the door with our luggage one bright November afternoon ! We had come to visit a training-home built in memory of good Bishop Tuttle, where twenty-five well-educated Negro girls were being prepared for social and welfare work. It lay in the grounds of the large Negro college of St. Augustine, at Raleigh, in North Carolina, one of the United States. Close by was a hospital, well-equipped and attractive, where Negro nurses were being trained. Teachers, nurses, and social workers were growing up side by side.

The place was full of life. Some students were coming back from a long morning of work in the houses and streets and outlying districts, others were just going out to the same work in the Community House for the afternoon. Some were writing up notes of the morning's lectures, others were preparing for to-morrow's classes. A few hours later the eager students gathered round us in the pleasant common room. We heard of those who had left the college after finishing their course and had gone out into work in town and country in many distant places. One and another told of the service to which she looked forward when her turn came to go, of the lectures she was attending, of the practical tasks she had in hand. These girls, for the sake of their own people, were studying questions of health and of housing, of food and of employment, of school work and of playgrounds and games. They were getting close to the mothers with their babies, and to the girls who met with so many temptations as they passed from childhood into womanhood. They were reading big books and hearing first-class lectures. Better still, they were learning love and wisdom by touching human life, and trying to understand the reasons why things went wrong. They went day by day from their happy training home into poor and neglected homes all round, caring for the feeble, relieving the needy, advising those who were puzzled, protecting those in moral danger, and teaching sad-faced children how to laugh and play. They hoped, when their training was over, to spend long years doing those same things in country or in town, working with town authorities, or with churches or social organisations.

We turn from this advanced training in North Carolina to Southern Rhodesia, to a little newly built village about a mile from Hope Fountain, where Rachel Masinga had her school (see p. 106). This little village is a " JEANES SCHOOL." There are many of these now in the United States where Miss Jeanes left money to help them, so they are called by her name. And there are several in Africa. This Jeanes School is new and small ; it has only women students. But it exactly meets the need of the people for whom it is built. As the women in the neighbouring kraals know very little, the school gives its students simple social training which will help the local home and community life.

The village has ten round huts for the students, a community room where they meet, a classroom for lectures, a pretty little hospital for their medical training, quarters for the teaching staff, and a kitchen and storeroom. The students are sent from various places to take the two years' course. They pass the fifth or sixth standard before they come, and generally have a fair working knowledge of English. Ten students, five married and five single, have completed the first two years' course.

PREPARING FOR SOCIAL SERVICE AT A JEANES SCHOOL

The students will have to work independently afterwards, so they are given a chance during their training to use their judgment and carry out treatments. They help in the in-patient and out-patient work in the little hospital. They sometimes treat and nurse cases out in the kraals, using only such things as the women have in their homes. They go in turn to the school each morning, examine cases, give treatments to some and report others to the hospital. Once a week a baby clinic is held, to which mothers from the neighbouring kraals bring their babies. Advice and treatment are free, and the weighing machine is an endless interest. On another day the kraal women come in and are taught sewing by the students. Once a week the students go out into different kraals.

Many industrial subjects are taught, and time is also found for gardening, basketry, and country dancing ; into this the students enter keenly. Bible study and Sunday school work find place, daily prayers are taken by the students in turn. Each woman is trained to keep a record of her daily work. In order to help them to teach others when they go to their future work, each student is given the needlework she has done and the patterns she has cut out. They also take with them simple books on mothercraft, health, and cookery and note books.

The great event of the year in this Jeanes School is the camp, when teachers and students go away for three or four weeks and get right out among the kraals. One year the whole party went up into the Matoppo Hills, to a place with the pretty name of Whitewater, about thirty miles from Hope Fountain. Each day they had a meeting in the village church, or in the kraal of a chief, or a teacher, or some of the women. From twenty to thirty women came to each meeting. In one place the chief came dressed in skins and wearing a hat with a feather. More than once the women were so shy that they ran and hid from the party.

A student took a short service, then a lesson or a demonstration on some practical subject was given. Perhaps it was a talk on personal cleanliness and a lesson on washing a coloured garment or taking out stains and spots. Many a day it was cooking for the sick, the women tasting, first with doubt and then with pleasure, the things which were made. One day they fought for the crumbs ! They were taught the way to prepare for the coming of a baby, how to treat a new-born infant—demonstrated with a doll—and how to wash a small child. Two tiny Africans greatly enjoyed real baths. The women learned to dress burns or sores, to bath eyes, to deal with snake-bites, and to make and use mealie-meal poultices. It took some time to teach how to cut out garments, for the women did not always know how to hold a pair of scissors. Everywhere these untaught women asked advice as to how they could make their huts better.

Pause and think for a moment what it means to have the wives and mothers in a district as ignorant and backward as this. In kraal after kraal they will hold back their husbands and children and be a drag on their advance. And then think what a noble life-work it would be to learn to help them, to get down beside them where they are and lead them onward step by step with patient love, the whole family following in their train.

Some of the finest human stuff in Africa is still buried in these unreached kraals and huts.

CHAPTER 12

THE FUTURE OF DAUGHTERS OF AFRICA

I

LEADERS IN RELIGIOUS LIFE

No chief in all Africa was more entirely Christian in his ways than Khama, head of the Bamangwato tribe. His first wife, Ma-Bessie, shone as a Christian mother and made the home of the chief full of the spirit of true religion. After her death Khama married Semane, also a splendid Christian home-maker. She cared for the great chief tenderly till he died. Khama's eldest son succeeded him, but died after a short unhappy reign. His little son, the new chief, was too young to rule, so Tsekedi, a son of Khama and Semane, was made regent. He followed in Khama's ways, with Semane, his mother, as counsellor and friend. It is another beautiful story of a woman's strong, wise influence in tribal affairs. Semane's picture opposite, taken only a year ago, shows what a capable gracious woman she is. Besides her share in public affairs, she is a vigorous temperance worker, carrying on Khama's battle against strong drink. She has wide influence among the women of the tribe. She goes amongst them and speaks to them at large meetings. She is a woman who counts in all the affairs of life.

This capacity for affairs, which African women have shown in the history of tribal life, is beginning to find scope in the Christian Church. At first African men were slow to recognise the value of

SEMANE, WIFE OF KHAMA THE GOOD

such women's aid. In Uganda, in the days of Bishop Tucker, a proposal to put a woman of the country on the committee that advised about education was simply laughed at by the synod— that is, the governing body of the Church. Who ever heard of a woman on a committee ! In 1928, however, the synod welcomed twelve European women among its members. Two years later twelve African women were added, without a single dissenting voice. It was a great and notable advance. One of the twelve is Mrs. Ham Mukasa, the Sekibobo's wife.

In the Teso country, to the east of Uganda, the women were quite down-trodden twenty years ago —of far less value than cattle. They were too depressed to want to improve their own position. The men, eager to read themselves, refused to let girls attend school and gave the first women readers many a beating. To-day the men are willing to pay fees for the education of their daughters, and there are nearly as many girls as boys in school.

Teso Christian women now have their monthly parish councils. They discuss all Church questions affecting women and girls. They are just in their decisions and business-like in their ways. The records of their councils are taken by two representatives to the men's councils, and any questions asked are answered. The Mothers' Union has come to Teso from Uganda, with much other help from the wives of the pastors and teachers sent by the Uganda Church. The Teso women, even those who still lack education, work the district branches well.

An Englishwoman, who went to West Africa in 1905, found in Lagos diocese a fine group of real women leaders connected with the Church. They backed up the missionaries, encouraged the teachers, visited the sick, and kept in touch with Church members who left the town. The youngest daughter of Bishop Crowther [1] was one of the group.

When a women's guild was formed for the Lagos diocese some fifteen years later, the women were given larger opportunities for united work. A women's diocesan conference is held every year, followed by conferences in the various districts. African women of experience give talks on practical questions. The Mothers' Union does strong work. West African women owe much to the untiring service of one of their own number, Mrs. Howells, wife of the Assistant Bishop on the Niger. She has never ceased to believe in the capacity of the women in the Niger Delta and has seen many of them respond to her teaching and fulfil her hopes.

Perhaps the most active guild or union among Christian women is the Manyano, which has branches in most of the Wesleyan churches in Southern Africa. The members, who number many thousands, wear a red blouse. They bind themselves to pray for the advance of the kingdom of God. They maintain a high standard of life. They help in the work of the local congregations. Sometimes, though far from rich, they combine to raise a large sum of money for some cause they have at heart. They go out and preach to the women in the kraals.

Would you like to see, through the eyes of a white woman who loves them, a great gathering of African women at prayer ?

" Our Bantu women recently took part in a world-wide day of prayer for women. A thousand

[1] *Lives of Eminent Africans*, pp. 65–77.

of them gathered in the largest Native church in Johannesburg. It was a wet and stormy afternoon, but nothing stopped the women. They came on foot, or in special buses, or by train from the outlying districts. It was an assembly full of colour. The uniforms of the women showed the Church to which they belonged. The red blouses of the Wesleyans blended with the black and white of the Presbyterians and, most picturesque of all, the leopard skin turbans of women from one of the American Methodist churches. It was a great, earnest gathering, quietly joining in prayer for the women of the world and especially for Bantu young people and children.

"As women leaders from the various churches rose to pray aloud, their poise, womanly dignity, and ability were most impressive. These Christian women are a mighty force for the coming of the kingdom of God in Africa."

Finally, there are just two women, out of the great crowd of Christian witnesses, whose stories will complete what has been said. The first is the story of the pastor's wife in a West African town. It is told by the friend who wrote about Margaret in an earlier chapter (see p. 77).

"We follow a little path leading round the church and find at the back a garden and a house that seems to say 'Welcome!' as you get near the door. The merry children run to tell their mother we have come. Presently we hear a rich voice full of pleasure and surprise, saying, 'Oh-ho-o' as the owner comes with outstretched hands to greet us. She is a great woman in more ways than one. Her personality matches her figure. She sheds confidence and calm about her as a lamp sheds light.

Her faith is as simple as that of a child. Her dignity is complete, but she never thinks about it. She is as able to lead as she is ready to follow.

" Her childhood was spent in a town full of superstition and heathen customs. Out of it she has grown into the gracious womanhood of a Christian wife and mother. She will listen gladly to a white woman, years younger than herself, trying with stumbling speech to address the women's meeting at the church. Or, if the white woman is not available, she will gather up the meeting into her own capable hands. She will lead the hymns. She will give the teaching more eloquently than any ' white one.' She will inspire the prayers. Finally, she will call three hundred names from the roll and put attendance marks against them in a great book.

" To her home come messengers from the sick and sorrowful, and from those who prosper and make merry. Friendliness and sympathy are there for joyful or for sad. There is about her an atmosphere of faith and gladness in which fears might shrink and wandering souls find steadiness and peace."

Here is the story of Wavatidé, a simple village evangelist. Queen Nzinga (p. 12) took us to the town of San Salvador in Portuguese Congo, as it was some four hundred years ago. The town is not so important now as it was then. But worthier daughters of Africa than Nzinga may be found there none the less. Wavatidé was one of these.

About fifty years ago missionaries came from England with their message. Many of the people believed what they said, among them was Wavatidé. She broke away from the fetishes and would believe in them no more. One day she went to a town and found a witch palaver going on. The medicine man had made a white circle on the ground and put a powerful fetish in the centre. He dared anybody to pass the circle or touch the fetish on pain of death. Wavatidé spoke out boldly. It was all lies, she said. God alone had the power of life and of death. Then she stepped into the middle of the circle, seized the fetish, and threw it into the bush. The people looked on, struck with horror. They expected to see Wavatidé fall dead before their eyes. But she quietly went on her way.

Wavatidé was an ignorant woman who never learned either to read or to write. But as an eager listener she learned the Gospel in her head and in her heart. Her life was like a book in which people could read the meaning of the Christian faith. Soon she began to go out into the villages in the district to repeat what she had learned. The people watched her and found that her life and her words fitted together; she was what she said. The tall, lean woman, with a bright face full of intelligence, had a tremendous influence in place after place. She died about ten years ago.

I wonder whether you agree with me that she deserves a place among African women leaders in religious life?

II

AFRICAN WOMEN AS MISSIONARIES

Christian people in America and Europe have sent out many missionaries to Africa. Some of the missionaries laid down their lives quite soon in Africa; others lived there for long and busy years.

But African Christians have been missionaries too. Here are the stories of Yona and Sabbath, who were both missionary wives.

When the Zulu Church of the American Board Mission was fifty years old a letter came to Umzumbe, down in Natal (pp. 89, 106), from English missionaries at Inyati, far north in Southern Rhodesia. The letter brought a big request. For twenty-five years the missionaries had been working and had seen little result. Could the Zulu Church send a preacher and his wife to help them ?

At a meeting of the Zulu Church the letter was read aloud. Eleven men rose and offered to go to Inyati. Among them was Mcitwa. This is what he said : " For many years I have been hearing about God's work in other lands. I have felt that if God ever called me I would go. I have not much education, but if the missionaries see fit, here am I, send me." Out of those who offered, Mcitwa, and his fine wife, Yona, were chosen to go.

They left their little two-year-old daughter with friends and took with them their baby son Elia, aged three weeks. They went by boat to Cape Town and from there by ox waggon to Inyati, a six months' trek. They followed the path taken by David Livingstone and suffered the same hardships. They felt the terrible thirst of travellers in the Kalahari desert. Sixteen times the waggons stuck fast, first in mud and then in sand. Mcitwa at last took the long ox-whip in his hands. Night after night he drove the span of oxen, helping to lift off the loads when the waggons stuck and put them on again. But the hardships of those six months ended, the husband and wife reached

Inyati. They have been called the Livingstones of the Zulu Church.

Mcitwa built a little house for his family. He only lived to preach three times. On the first Sunday night, though fever was on him, he spoke to the congregation for an hour. But the toil of the journey had broken his strength ; he lay down on his bed and died.

A few days later Baby Elia also died of fever. The graves of the father and the little son lie there in far Inyati. It is like the story of the white missionary, Dr. Krapf, who landed at Mombasa to bear his message inland in East Africa. In a few days he laid his wife and infant daughter in their grave.

Yona waited on alone at Inyati, her strong, sweet character shining through the cloud of her grief. At last a British official travelling southward offered to take care of her on her long journey home. She reached Umzumbe two years and two months after she and Mcitwa and the baby boy had left. She had gone out full and came back empty. In less than a year Yona too got ill and died, leaving the little daughter Amy as the only living member of the first missionary family of the Zulu Church in Umzumbe.

Here is a story of two African missionaries, man and wife, from the Transvaal. It has been written for us by the English Bishop of St. Albans, who was once Bishop of Pretoria and has never forgotten his African friends.

" An African man from Sekukuniland, in the North-East Transvaal, went away to work for a white man and was converted to the Christian faith. At baptism he took the name of Job. After a time he returned home. Sunday after

Sunday he stood under an old tree in the village of Mooifontein and preached the Gospel—so far as he knew it—to the heathen folk. Again and again messages came down to Pretoria asking that a teacher might be sent up, but there were neither funds nor men. At last dear old Job died. In 1917 I was able to send up a Native deacon, Thulo, but just as he was beginning to learn the local language, Sepedi, and getting his work started, he was stricken down with influenza in the bad epidemic of 1918 and died.

" I felt that at all costs I must find a man to take his place. After much thought I sent for Augustine Moeka, who was then a young priest in the Native Mission in Pretoria. I told him of the need ; I asked him if he would go. He was quite frank, he did not wish to do so ; the language was to him a strange language ; the people were foreigners ; Sekukuniland was a very long way off. Besides he was engaged to be married to the school teacher at Pretoria, Sabbath by name. How was he to take her so far away ? ' But,' he said, ' if you, my lord, tell Augustine he must go, Augustine will go.' ' And,' I added, ' so will Sabbath, for she too has the right spirit.' So it was that Augustine and Sabbath became man and wife and set out on their new and twofold adventure. I never had one moment's doubt that the two of them together would make good, and they have.

" Augustine had known as a boy something of what real persecution means at the hands of those Africans who angrily resent one of their own people adopting the white man's religion, more especially if the man in question comes from a chief's family, as Augustine did. Both he and

Sabbath have learnt more of what persecution means since they have lived and worked together away up in Sekukuniland, but together they have faced it for themselves and their people, and have turned it to good account. They have undoubtedly met with great disappointments, but they have been the means of setting before their people an amazingly high standard of devotion, and real dependence, through prayer, on the power of the Holy Spirit.

" In the seventeen years that I knew the Transvaal and was in close touch with the Native work, I have never known any African woman who was so clearly suited to be a priest's wife, or one who has so wonderfully risen to her calling as Sabbath. I love to think of that partnership between her and Augustine, in their home, in the school, in their common life of devotion and prayer, in their courage and patience, in the face of persecution and disappointment, in their enthusiastic loyalty to our Blessed Lord, and in their complete devotion to the people among whom their lot is cast. It is a wonderful partnership between a Christian gentleman and a Christian lady.

" Sabbath is the first African woman to attain the rank of Leader of the Wayfarers, an organisation corresponding to the Girl Guides. They tell me that when Princess Alice came to inspect a great gathering of Wayfarers in Johannesburg, the honour of making a little speech of thanks was entrusted to Sabbath, and that she did it—as I can well believe—with all the grace and natural dignity of one who might have done it all her life.

" When I think of Augustine and Sabbath in their home and work in Sekukuniland, I take heart and hope, and thank God for Christian missions in Africa."

It is eleven years since the Bishop who writes this story has seen Padre Augustine and Sabbath his wife. But their faithful work goes on.

III

OUTLOOK

A great company of African women have passed before us in these pages. How varied they have been—queens and woman chiefs and little slave girls ; women educated in African schools or overseas, and women unable even to read ; honoured wives and mothers in prosperous homes, and women left homeless and without their husbands in the hard fight of life. Some of them are known to history ; others are hidden in the circle of their friends. It is a great roll of honour ; it might be made ten times as long.

Worth of character is the standard by which we have measured all these women. We do not claim that all African women are either capable or good. Africa has as large a proportion of unsatisfactory daughters as the rest of the human family. Groups of poor, down-trodden African women still live in surroundings where they have no chance to rise. In Africa, as elsewhere, many women have chosen evil when they might have chosen good. All that is true. Nevertheless, after the stories told here it is safe to say, quite boldly, that African women, as a whole, have at least as much character and capacity as African men.

Now every onward path has its dangers. This has been clearly seen in the modern advance of

women in every land. Sometimes barriers have
been put across the women's path. Sometimes
side paths have tempted the women themselves to
turn aside from the true straight way.

In Africa there is danger lest the men should
block the women's onward way. Men naturally
and rightly want to keep the finer womanly qualities
shown in old African life. The capable service
which women have given is too good to lose. But
the way to secure it is not by shutting women out
from a full share in the new day which men are
entering themselves. Home has no liberty and
social life has no richness or beauty where men
move forward and women are left behind. Here
are some true incidents which show that in Africa
this danger is still great.

A new resident met a couple belonging to a
South African tribe on a country road. The
husband walked in front, swinging a cane in his
hand. His wife followed wearily, laden with
bundles, a child dragging at her side. " Why,"
said the white man, moved to indignation, " do
you let your wife carry all that load for you ? "
The husband paused in amazement. " Whose
wife would carry it for me if my own did not ? "
It never occurred to him that he might carry it
himself. That has been a common way in Africa
for hundreds of years.

Not long ago a young white man and his wife
called upon an English-speaking chief south of the
Zambesi. They found a pleasant intelligent man
in English dress. He invited them to dine with
him. They sat at a table set with knives and forks.
The food was brought in by two nearly naked
women, wives of the chief, who, on their knees,

moved with it across the floor. The chief had no idea what his guests felt about this.

An African on the staff of a mission invited a white worker to see his home. He pointed with satisfaction to a small European bed. " I sleep there," he said. " And where does your wife sleep ? " asked the visitor. " On the floor underneath," was the reply.

A trusty African worker married a nice girl from the mission school. " I hope," said a foreign member of the staff, " that you will treat your wife as your equal and not make her eat only after you." " I have no objection to eating with her," he replied, " but she would not like it till she is quite tame." " How long will that take ? " He answered, " About a year."

A recent traveller looked out of the train at a railway station far inland in the Belgian Congo. On the platform was a mother seeing off her son. He was a smart little brown lad in shorts and a jersey, with a peaked cap such as Belgian boys wear. He probably spoke French and was on his way to school down the river. His mother was almost naked, a woman belonging only to the bush. Life held some problems for the future of that mother and son.

The greatest barrier to the progress of the African woman is the practice of polygamy. Some women still accept it without protest, because each extra wife means a division of the heavy work in house and in garden. Other girls and women turn away from it and even resist it with all their might. In some districts poverty has lessened polygamy, for wives cost money to procure and to maintain. Here and there governments discourage it, as contrary to the welfare of the population. The

Christian Church as a whole has steadily opposed it, though weak Christians fall into the practice at times, and some African religious bodies permit it. Polygamy can only be dealt with by the free action of African men. Until they condemn it, judging it as unworthy of their helpmates and of themselves, it will not pass away, for its roots lie deep in the weakness of human nature and are embedded in the customs of the race.

The seclusion of women is not a general custom in Africa. But it prevails in parts. Take an instance of it at its very best. There is in a Moslem region of Africa a ruler with many wives. He is a kindly, cultured man. In his great house each wife has her own apartment and is allowed to see certain women friends. Among the frequent visitors is a young white woman, who has found in the big household an intimate and loyal friend in one of the ruler's wives. " If I were in a tight place," she says, " I would as soon have her with me as anyone I know. There is something so big and true and sane about her. She seems to have such a generous and broad outlook on humanity, with its weaknesses and good points." This able and charming woman is shut in to a single household, one of many wives who spend their days within its walls. She can have no touch with the life all round her. Is the system fair to so fine a woman ? Is it fair that Africa should lose the service of a daughter who could do so much ?

Among educated African men, especially those who have studied in Western lands, many are thirsting to know the equal fellowship which some of their best white friends find in married life. A young African was examining a book written by a white man he knew. In the preface the author acknowledged that the book could not have been written without the help and criticism of his wife. The African said sadly, " I know of no African writer who could have stated. that." Africans of the new generation and those who love them cannot rest until this situation is met. A beginning has already been made in the opening of excellent girls' schools. But much more needs to be done. The United States of America is leading the way in the equal educational opportunities provided for women in its Negro group.

So much for the barriers which lie across the women's onward way. Women themselves, in Western lands and in Asia as well as in Africa, have often hindered their own advance. Side paths have led them out of the true way. Good things they might well have kept were left behind them ; things of little use were eagerly grasped. Some of the mistakes made in Africa are due to the failure of white friends to perceive in early days the riches of African life.

In all that is best in literature and art—in all the finest things in the world—Africa's daughters have as truly a share as the women of other lands. But Africa has also a heritage which is all her own to enjoy and to share. African beauty, African art and music, African names, African languages which enshrine a people's soul, are too precious to be abandoned and thrown aside.

The liberty of the new day, when ancient bondage is lifted from the woman's shoulders, should purify but not destroy the spirit of that community life in which Africa is so rich. There are aspects of tribal discipline and respect for elders which fathers and mothers may carry forward into modern home life, and which educated African women may preserve in social and professional service. The educated African woman will never become a mere individual if she is true to the genius of her race. She will rejoice without doubt that the heavy age-long burden of field work and household toil is lightened, yet she will recall with pride the ancient marriage gift—from husband to wife—of a hoe. Some can actually join with such women as the Sekibobo's wife in maintaining their historic place in the work of the garden and the home. Nothing will more ennoble the future than a combination of the best elements and characteristics of old Africa with the gifts of the new day.

Even in the dress of its women Africa will lose if she wholly forsakes her past and copies from other lands. The lack of modest covering, the cutting of tribal marks or the painting of the body with designs full of meaning, the loading of face and limbs with heavy ornaments—these are things to be left behind. But in parts of Africa the ordinary dress of the women is full of grace and beauty. An appreciation of this has recently been written by a brilliant young Englishman sent to Africa on official work.

" It is the Native women of Kampala (Uganda) who attract most attention. They walk abroad leisurely and dignified, their glistening and beautifully shaped shoulders rising bare above a long robe, gathered at one side, that falls from breast to feet. In old days the robes were as modest as now, and of the same general pattern but made of bark cloth. To-day, however, the women wear cotton prints, or, if they can afford them, the most radiant silks or even velvets. It is an unforgettable sight to see a Baganda woman, with her soft rounded features and close-cropped head, advancing towards you, her chocolate skin in perfect contrast with a blue velvet or daffodil silk."

African women often look charming in Western dress and choose it with perfect taste as to style and colour. In many places it is the only natural thing for them to wear. But certain Western fashions, which are extreme, extravagant, and ungraceful, are copied by African girls in country places or in towns, from fashion books or from some gaily attired European woman. It is not merely beauty that is lost. With the fashions inexperienced and undisciplined young people copy what they believe to be the social customs and dances of white folk. They get into loose ways and undesirable company. Many, as the wisest African mothers tell us, have fallen into moral peril through turning down such a path.

One last word. What of coming days?

While hope rises high for Africa and its people no one can fail to see the storm-clouds in the sky. Racial unrest spreads from one area to another, even into country parts. Questions of land and labour are always anxious, sometimes acute. Poverty is deep. At times, and in certain places, fear, discontent, distrust, and even hatred break into the relations of those who should live together in friendship and mutual trust. Human force may hold back the outbreak of unrest. But only one thing can touch the source of trouble and make what is bitter sweet. When there is built up in Africa, secretly and by hidden ways, a spiritual kingdom of righteousness, peace, and joy, then the land will have rest. Black and white races will in honour prefer one another. Old injustices and resentments will be put right and forgiven. Material gain will fall into a second place. The spirit of love which can bring this great thing to pass has been released in Africa, and it works.

Meantime the stress and strain of the present situation press heavily on the mind and temper of African men. It is a harder battle than their fathers' tribal wars. Can the women of Africa come to their aid ?

In a record of the past we read that when the tribesmen were out at battle the women at home kept peace, lest quarrels between them should weaken the men at the front. A chief's wife during a battle would sit on a struggling sheep or on an earthenware pot to signify her hope that her husband was holding down or enclosing his foes. Thus African women shared in the issues of the conflict.

A nobler share in a greater conflict is theirs to-day. A woman can soothe her husband's spirit and calm him by her faith in the slow, sure justice of God and in the love of white folk, her friends, who are working for Africa. A mother can train up her sons and daughters to be worthy of a liberty and opportunity hitherto withheld from their race. Worth will win more than the best-directed agitation, as the Negroes in the United States have proved. And home, the women's stronghold, is the place where worth is bred and perfected.

A woman who seeks after righteousness and peace in her home will be a true Daughter of Africa, in the great line of the best of those whose stories are told in this book.

INDEX

(The names of those whose stories are told are printed in SMALL CAPITALS.)